Dr Catherine Dawson has been a researcher specializing in educational research, and a tutor working with college and university students for over twenty-five years. She is passionate about helping students to succeed on their courses. She is also the author *of Introduction to Research Methods* and *Advanced Research Methods.*

D0177110

Also by Dr Catherine Dawson

Introduction to Research Methods
Advanced Research Methods

BASIC STUDY SKILLS

Dr Catherine Dawson

howtobooks

Practical books that inspire

OLDHAM METRO LIBRARY SERVICE	
A34144992	
Bertrams	16/08/2013
A371.30281	£9.99
OLD	

Constable & Robinson Ltd
55-56 Russell Square
London WC1B 4HP
www.constablerobinson.com

First published in the UK as *The Complete Study Skills Guide* by How To Books Ltd., 2011

Published in this edition by How To Books, an imprint of Constable & Robinson Ltd., 2013

Copyright © Catherine Dawson 2011

The right of Catherine Dawson to be identified as the author of this work has been asserted by her in accordance with the Copyright, Designs & Patents Act 1988.

All rights reserved. This book is sold subject to the condition that it shall not, by way of trade or otherwise, be lent, re-sold, hired out or otherwise circulated in any form of binding or cover other than that in which it is published and without a similar condition including this condition being imposed on the subsequent purchaser.

A copy of the British Library Cataloguing in Publication

Data is available from the British Library

ISBN 978-1-8452-8520-3 (paperback)
ISBN 978-1-4721-1009-1 (ebook)

Printed and bound by CPI Group (UK) Ltd, Croydon, CR0 4YY

1 3 5 7 9 10 8 6 4 2

Contents

Preface

This book has been written for students who wish to improve their study skills. It is aimed at the following types of student:

- school pupils studying for A levels and vocational qualifications;

- students studying at further education and community colleges;

- overseas students;

- adults studying on adult education courses;

- adults studying at residential colleges;

- undergraduate students studying at university;

- distance, correspondence and online learners.

The book covers all aspects of study skills, from improving reading, writing, listening and thinking skills, to knowing how to study independently, conduct research and take tests and examinations.

It has been written in a user-friendly, accessible format that enables you to dip in and out of the book whenever you need to brush up on a particular skill. It also includes useful exercises, addresses, websites and further reading for those who wish to follow up the information provided in the book.

Tip People are not born with the ability to study well. It is a skill that can be learned by anyone who wants to succeed on their course.

I have been a tutor and researcher working in further education colleges, universities and adult residential colleges for over twenty-five years. The quotations, case studies, tips and exercises have been collected over that period and during recent research with college and university students.

I understand that many students, in particular those from non-traditional backgrounds, are anxious about their ability to study well and succeed on their course. However, all students can learn how to study well: it is not a skill reserved for the select few. This book has been written with those concerns in mind. It provides a practical, 'how to' approach that can be followed by any student who is keen to improve their study skills.

Tip Keep this book by your side throughout your studies. It will be useful for every stage of your course.

I hope that you find this book useful and interesting and that you are able to refer to it often throughout your course. I wish you every success with your studies.

1 Developing your learning skills

All students need to develop their learning skills to be successful in their studies. It is important that you gain an awareness of how you learn, as this will help you to make the right learning choices, improve your ability to learn and help you to develop your study skills. It will also help you to understand how to improve your memory, concentration and intellectual capacity. These issues are discussed in this chapter.

Understanding how to learn

Learning is not just about memorizing facts. It also includes the development of skills, knowledge, critical thinking and power of argument. Learning also helps us to carry out tasks more successfully and efficiently. There are three main types of learning.

- Learning that helps you to improve your physical abilities. For example, at school you may have been taught how to play football or hockey. Or you may have been taught how to swim as a child. Indeed, as a very young child you learned how to stand, walk, run and skip.

- Learning that helps you to develop and increase your knowledge. Everything you know has been learned at some stage in your life.

Learning that helps you to change your attitude and beliefs. This could be in a formal learning setting, such as school or college, or you may have experienced a situation that tested your existing assumptions, helped you to learn something new and changed your attitudes.

Exercise

Think about your own experiences of learning in relation to the three types described above. Identify the situations in which you consider your learning to have been successful and unsuccessful. Consider the reasons for success and failure.

Succeeding to learn

When I have worked through the above exercise with students at college and university it becomes clear that, for successful learning to take place, the following should occur:

- The skills to be learned are relevant to you and your needs;
- You are interested in your learning;
- You are motivated to learn;
- You can learn to use these skills in different contexts and activities;
- You are actively involved in the learning process;
- You are able to think, develop and work at your own pace;
- You feel comfortable in your learning environment;
- You are comfortable with the tutor, teaching methods and/ or teaching materials.

If you enrol on a course that meets the criteria for successful learning, you will find that you enjoy the course and are motivated to learn. As a consequence, you should be more successful in your studies.

Failing to learn

However, from the above exercise you will have identified some of the reasons for unsuccessful learning. These can include:

- poor teaching methods and/or materials;
- uncomfortable learning environment;
- lack of time;
- lack of confidence;
- low opinion of self and ability;
- stress and anxiety;
- lack of motivation and interest;
- irrelevance to life and interests;
- being forced to do something you don't want to do.

It is important to be aware that some of these reasons are due to external factors that may be difficult for you to overcome, such as poor teaching methods and materials. If this is the case you need to discuss the issues with your tutor/teacher or think about moving to a more appropriate course.

Becoming a reflective learner

In addition to the points discussed above, you will become more successful in your learning if you develop your skills of reflection.

Reflective thought involves the ability to acquire facts, understand ideas and arguments, apply methodological principles,

analyse and evaluate information, weigh evidence and produce conclusions and/or persuasive arguments. It includes the
ability to question and solve problems by linking your previous ideas, knowledge and experiences with present ideas,
knowledge and experiences.

The following points will help you to think more about how to
become a reflective learner.

- Your ability to reflect increases as you create mental challenges for yourself through creating tasks, setting
  objectives and engaging in activities such as reading and
  writing.
- Social interaction aids reflection. Discussions with like-
  minded people, students and tutors will help you to reflect
  on what you are learning.
- Reflection becomes easier the more you know about a
  topic.
- Reflection is more effective if carried out in an appropriate
  environment free from distraction.
- Constructive feedback helps your ability to reflect.
- Writing down your ideas helps. Your writing can be
  descriptive, but should also include personal judgement,
  personal discourse and an analysis of outside influences on
  your thought processes and development of arguments.

Understanding how you reflect

Reflection takes place at different speeds, levels and intens-
ities. For example, when you are first presented with an idea
you may find that you reflect rapidly on what is being said.
After the speaker has finished you might evaluate quickly,
forming your own ideas.

Later you might think about the ideas in more depth, slowly, taking your time. Then you might return to the idea at a later date, when something else reminds you of what you have learned. At this time you are able to bring in new ideas that help to build on what you have learned previously.

Tip Becoming a reflective learner is a skill that is cultivated over time. You will get better as your course progresses.

Training your body and mind to learn

One of the most important aspects of training your mind to learn is to recognize and take control of those factors that distract you from your learning. These vary, depending on your learning environment, your personal motivation, your likes and dislikes and your personal circumstances. Examples of the type of distractions that may affect your learning are listed in Table 1.

Table 1. Learning distractions.

Emotional	Physical	Psychological	Sociological
Lack of confidence	Mobility problems	Fear of failure	Unable to work in groups
Lack of motivation	Poor eyesight	Low self-esteem	Difficult to bond with fellow students
Lack of interest	Poor hearing	Deflated ego	No connection with tutor
Feelings of nervousness or anxiety	Health problems	Feelings of alienation or being 'out of place'	Unfamiliar learning environment

---

Exercise

Think carefully about the factors that could distract you from your studies. Make a list of these distractions and decide what strategies you intend to use to overcome the problems.

Recognizing your learning style

Over recent years a great deal has been written about individual learning styles and there are now various models available (see further reading on page 12). Some people believe that the learning styles that you were born with remain the same throughout your life, whereas others believe learning styles can and will change as you grow older. Others believe that we use different styles for different types of learning.

Today, on the internet, there are a variety of surveys that help you to start thinking about your preferred learning style. Enter 'learning style survey' into your search engine and have a go at completing a few surveys. It is an interesting exercise as it makes you think about the way you retain information. However, you should remember that this type of online survey can be open to misinterpretation and error, so don't take the results too seriously.

Learning style questions

A popular learning style model was created by Neil Fleming (www.vark-learn.com), expanding on ideas that had been developed within the field of neurolinguistic programming (www.anlp.org). The following questions will help you to think more about your learning style, based on Fleming's model.

1. Do you prefer to learn with other people, perhaps in a group or team? This would indicate a social/interpersonal learning style.

2. Do you prefer to work alone? This would indicate a solitary/intrapersonal learning style.

3. Do you prefer using pictures, images and visualization? This would indicate a visual/spatial learning style.

4. Do you prefer using sound and music? This would indicate an aural/auditory learning style.

5. Do you prefer using words in both speech and writing? This would indicate a verbal/linguistic learning style.

6. Do you prefer using your sense of touch? This would indicate a physical/kinesthetic learning style.

7. Do you prefer using logic, reason and systematic thinking? This would indicate a logical/mathematical learning style.

Most people have a mix of the learning styles described above, although one, probably, will be more dominant than the other. If you are able to recognize your dominant and/or preferred learning style(s), you can choose learning techniques that will help you to study more effectively and successfully.

Tip An awareness of your learning style can help to steer you towards the right type of course/module. It can also help you to avoid courses where there is a mismatch between the teaching style of your tutor and your preferred learning style.

Improving concentration and memory

Our memory is made up of two main parts: the short-term memory and the long-term memory. In the short-term memory we store facts and ideas for as long as we need to apply them. In the long-term memory we store information that we will use at a later stage.

To pass information from the short-term memory to the long-term memory we have to practise what we have learned. This involves careful reflection and analysis, thinking about what we have learned, writing about the concepts and ideas and understanding them. It may also involve some form of repetition and rote learning, especially in the case of facts and figures.

Tip   Remember that almost everybody can improve their memory. In most cases people do not have a bad memory – they just use their memory badly.

Developing an effective memory

There are four parts to developing an effective memory.

- Information is received through our senses: hearing, sight, touch, smell and taste. However, to receive information effectively, we must be open to receiving the information. This means that it must have some personal relevance and we must be paying attention to what we are receiving.

- The information is stored in our memory in an effective manner. This will depend on the type of information we are receiving. Facts and figures may have to be repeated over and over again, ideas and concepts may have to be thought about, written about and discussed. The storage of information is more effective if we understand what we are storing.

- The information has to be stored in an appropriate place within our memory. This involves a process of organization during which ideas are related to each other. It is easier to remember things if we can relate it to past experience and knowledge.

- We must be able to retrieve the information when it is required. This may involve practice in recalling information and regularly reviewing the information we have stored.

Learning style and memory

As we have seen earlier, people learn in different ways. This affects the way we remember; for example, visual learners will find it easier to remember faces whereas linguistic learners will find it easier to remember names.

Your memory, therefore, can be improved by understanding the learning style that helps you to take in and retain the information in the most effective way. This means that, depending on your learning style, you can use visual, auditory or tactile modes of learning to help you to remember information and to add interest to your studies.

Tips for improving memory

Pay attention.

Stay motivated.

Understand what you wish to remember.

Relate the information to what you already know.

Find an interest in the material to be remembered.

Commit information to memory using a learning mode that suits your learning style.

Use rhymes, acronyms, pictures, stories and songs to help you to remember.

Involve as many senses as possible.

Organize the information into related and/or relevant categories.

Practise, rehearse and 'over-learn' information such as dates and figures.

Write about and discuss ideas, themes and concepts.
Avoid cramming information.
Take regular breaks when memorizing.
Vary your memorizing routine.
Retrieve information from your memory on a regular basis.
Relate retrieved information to new information.

Using your brain effectively

Over the years there has been an enormous amount of research into brain function and activity. If this is an area of study that interests you, see further reading on page 12.

You will find that you can begin to use your brain more effectively if you take note of the following advice.

- Keep your brain active and exercised. Develop your analytical and critical thinking skills. Don't believe everything you are told. Digest, analyse and reform ideas and arguments (see Chapter 8).

- Give your brain challenges. Try online brain tools and/or tackle crossword puzzles, Sudoku, basic (or more advanced) maths puzzles, card games and other games that require you to develop your powers of induction, deduction and complex strategy.

- Try to learn something new as often as possible. However, you should make sure that this does not become a mental chore. Learning should be fun.

- Get plenty of physical exercise as this can help brain function and some people believe that it may reduce the risk of developing brain disorders, such as dementia, in later life.

- Eat a balanced, healthy diet. Studies show that a diet rich in nutrients such as antioxidants and vitamins boosts brain function and memory. Make sure that you always eat breakfast as this raises mental and physical energy levels.

Using memory and brain improvement tools

Recently, there has been a massive surge in the popularity of brain-training tools and technology. However, researchers are still undecided about the effectiveness of these tools. Therefore, you will need to decide for yourself as to whether any tools you use are helping to improve your memory and brain function.

There are a wide variety of free tools available on the internet. Enter 'brain training games' to be directed to various sites that provide free brain-training games. Some of these are fun and interesting to complete, but as with anything you find on the internet, make sure that it is a legitimate site and that you don't give personal details or hand over any cash (see Chapter 13 for more information about e-learning tools).

In addition to these free games there are an increasing number of brain-training games available for purchase. Again, researchers are not sure about how effective these games are and some believe that they are no better than the simple, free activities described above. Therefore, as a student you might be better saving your money.

Summary

If you are to succeed in your studies it is important to understand how you learn, as this will help you to improve your brain function, concentration and memory. You can also increase your chances of success by becoming a reflective learner and keeping a record of your progress. The most important way to keep your brain functioning well is to keep physically and mentally healthy and active.

Once you have started to develop your learning skills, you need to think about practical issues of organization. It is important to organize your studies as this will help you to enjoy your course, increase motivation and help you to succeed. These issues are discussed in the following chapter.

Further reading

Al-Chalabi, A. et al., *The Brain: A beginner's guide* (Oxford: Oneworld Publications, 2008).

Greenfield, S., *The Human Brain: A guided tour* (London: Phoenix, 2001).

Kolb, D., *Experiential Learning: Experience as the source of learning and development* (Englewood Cliffs, NJ: Prentice-Hall, 1984).

Moon, J., *A Handbook of Reflective and Experiential Learning: Theory and practice* (London: Routledge, 2004).

2 Learning to be organized

All students need to develop their organization skills if they are to succeed in their studies. This involves the ability to manage your time and effectively juggle work, study and your social life. It is also important that you plan your study carefully and make sure that you meet all coursework deadlines.

If you are able to do this successfully you will find that you enjoy your studies, are more motivated to learn and will improve your chances of success. These issues are discussed in this chapter.

Managing your time

Time management is all about taking control of your own time. The following advice will help you to do this.

- Draw up a list of non-negotiable activities that you must carry out each week. This will include attending lectures, seminars and tutorials, and any other essential activities.

- Set aside some time for private study. Try to do this at a time that suits the way you like to work. Make sure that partners, friends or family know that you shouldn't be disturbed at this time.

- Set a clear start and stop time for your study sessions. You will find that you begin to work faster but don't lose any understanding of the material.

▪ Think of the most efficient way to carry out a task or cope with a problem. Many student hours are wasted trying to sort out a computer problem or find a particular reference in the library. Ask an expert instead.

▪ Recreation and socializing are important for your frame of mind and well-being, but remember that work and play don't mix. When you are relaxing don't think about work, and when you are working, don't think about what you will be doing at the weekend.

▪ Don't work at a time when you should be sleeping. Sleep is essential for your intellectual, emotional and physical health (see Chapter 22).

Tip Avoid marathon study sessions. Shorter sessions tend to be more productive, especially when committing material to memory.

Time-wasting activities

Students at colleges and universities were asked what they considered to be their worst time-wasting activities. These included:

▪ surfing the net for irrelevant material;

▪ answering and sending unimportant e-mail;

▪ texting;

▪ gaming;

▪ spending time on social networking sites;

▪ searching for and reading irrelevant material in the library;

▪ chatting with friends and family on their mobile;

▪ worrying or fretting unnecessarily;

- trying to sort out computer hardware or software problems;
- putting off assignments by filling time with mundane and unimportant activities;
- watching television and/or listening to music;
- feeling ill/lying in bed due to too much socializing and drinking;
- waiting for assignments/other material to print.

Exercise

Choose a week at the beginning of your course. Make a list of all the ways that you think you have wasted time during this week, using the list above as a guide. (It is best to choose a week at the beginning of term because you will be able to develop good habits from the start of your course and you will be less busy with coursework at this time.) Jot down an action plan that will help you to get rid of these time-wasting activities.

In the next week use this action plan to change these activities, keeping a record so that you know whether or not you have been successful. If you haven't been successful, continue for a third week, working hard to reduce time-wasting activities.

Through careful action and monitoring, you will find that your habits begin to change over a few weeks, and that you become more efficient with your time.

Juggling work, study and play

As we have seen above, a social life is very important. Indeed, researchers believe that social interaction has an extremely positive influence on brain development and function (see Chapter 1). Therefore, you should not neglect your social life while you are studying, but you need to make sure that it does not take over to the detriment of your studies.

Also, you must make sure that your socializing does not have an adverse influence on your physical and mental well-being. As a student, you understand that too many late nights, alcohol and drugs will not help you to be top of the class.

Working during your studies

Recent research by the National Union of Students (NUS) and HSBC found that 64% of students had, or intended to take on, paid employment during the academic year, with 32% of these opting for term-time jobs. For some students this need to work is due to financial necessity, whereas for others it is to gain valuable work experience.

Whether you need to work through necessity, or whether you choose to work in paid employment, you must make sure that your employment does not have an adverse influence on your studies.

University regulations

Some colleges and universities have regulations about the number of hours a week you are able to spend in paid employment during term-time if you are a full-time student. These limits are provided in an attempt to make sure that your employment does not distract you too much from your studies (the NUS/HSBC survey reported that 43% of working students said that employment had affected their studies).

If you are thinking about obtaining a job you must find out whether your university or college has regulations about working hours. Contact your students' union or the university student employment service for further information.

Completing coursework and meeting deadlines

The following points will help you to think about meeting deadlines and handing in work on time.

- At the beginning of your course you should be given a timetable that includes all the assignment and project deadlines. Familiarize yourself with these dates, using a wall calendar (these can be obtained from students' union shops) or electronic calendar.

- Complete all assignments at least three days before the deadline. That way you won't be held up by unforeseen problems such as printer queues or computer crashes.

- Don't procrastinate. The definition of 'procrastinate' is to defer, to delay from day to day. Don't put off your work. When you need to complete a piece of work for your course, start as soon as possible.

- If you find that you are having problems completing your work, stop and do something else for a while. You will find it easier to approach your work refreshed. If you start each assignment early enough, you will have plenty of time to do this.

- Hand in assignments on time, even if they are not perfect or complete. You will still get some marks and the work might not be as bad as you think. Some tutors will have strict rules about late submissions and will award a '0' mark if you don't have a very good reason for late submission.

Tip Talk over study problems with fellow students or your tutor. Often you will find that another mind helps you to overcome your block.

Preparing a study plan

A study plan is a strategy that you can use to help you to achieve the most from your studies. Use the steps below to help you to prepare your study plan.

Step 1: Set your goals

A goal is a clear statement that describes what you will be able to do at the end of your studies. This will include specific behaviour and clear outcomes. It is useful to set goals so that you can keep your studies on track and make sure that, on completion, you have achieved what you hoped to have achieved. More information about setting goals is provided in Chapter 22.

Tip Consult your course introductory literature to check that the 'course outcomes' or 'learning outcomes' match your personal goals. If not, you need to decide whether there might be a more appropriate course available.

Step 2: List your study tasks

This should include all the tasks that you will be required to undertake as part of your course, and could include tasks such as memorizing information, learning facts, reading books, analysing books, writing assignments, and so on.

Step 3: List potential study problems

Go through your list of study tasks and note any that you think will create problems. Include any other problems that you think you may have with your studies, such as lack of interest and motivation, or too much emphasis on your social life.

Step 4: Rectify study problems

Once you have listed potential problems, think about the action you need to take to rectify the problems. Some problems will need specific action, whereas others can be overcome as your course progresses and your skills improve.

Step 5: Identify your strengths and weaknesses

Through identifying your strengths and weaknesses you can work out which parts of the course will be easy to complete and you can highlight any potential problem areas. This will enable you to think about coping strategies before the problems escalate. It is useful to think about your strengths as it helps you to feel positive about your ability to complete the course, and will help you to realize that some tasks can be completed easily.

Step 6: Develop a semester/term plan

Using your course materials and other information supplied by your tutor, find out what tasks you will need to complete by the end of the semester or term. As we have seen above, enter any important dates and study tasks that need completing onto a wall or electronic calendar so that you don't miss any deadlines (see quotation below).

'I got a wall calendar from the students' union, stuck it on my bedroom wall and filled it in in bright colours, different colours for different things like, you know, lectures were red, seminars were yellow, assignment deadlines were green...I could also write in other stuff, you know, like parties and stuff. I put them all on 'cos then I could see it from my bed, you know, as soon as I got up, then I didn't miss anything...It was a bit mad, you know, a bit hectic, but it worked for me.'

Louise, Bournemouth University.

Using task and time management software

Today there is a wide variety of task and time management software available to help you manage your time more effectively. Functions that are available include:

- preparing time management plans;
- clarifying what you need to do;
- prioritizing your time;
- setting goals;
- predicting what you need to do;
- monitoring your time;
- scheduling your time;
- analysing how you spend your time.

If you are a competent user you will find that this software will help you to become much more efficient with your time. However, if you are unsure of the technology, you need to make sure that getting to grips with the features does not take up too much of your valuable time.

Some of the software is free: enter 'free time management software' into your search engine to be directed to some useful sites. If you are intending to buy software you need to undertake careful research to make sure that it will meet your needs. Alternatively, contact your IT services department at your college or university to find out what is available for students to use free of charge (see Chapter 12 for more information about IT facilities in colleges and universities).

Overcoming organization problems

If you feel that you have problems with personal organization, don't bury your head in the sand. The sooner you acknowledge that you have a problem, the sooner you can take action (see quotation below). Early action will also alleviate associated problems, such as stress, anxiety and an inability to complete coursework and meet deadlines.

> *'I really started to panic. She [the tutor] was really helpful though... She got me to calm down and talk about it all. Then she gave me an extension...I think they're very good like that with mature students. I don't know whether all places do that. But it helped. It stopped me panicking and I got a bit calmer. When you panic you can't write anything, it all just goes out of the window...So I would say always go to your tutor. They're quite human really and they sort of, you know, well, they put it into perspective really.'*
>
> Alison, Sheffield Hallam University

As we have seen in the quotation above, if you find that poor organization is having a detrimental influence on your studies, speak to your tutor. Many colleges and universities offer additional training courses for students to help them to improve their organizational skills. Others will provide information leaflets or tailored advice and guidance to students who are struggling to cope (see Appendix 2 for more information about the type of study skills support that is available in colleges and universities).

Maximizing productivity

If you take note of the advice and guidance offered in this chapter you should find that you are able to better organize your studies, take control of your time and increase your productivity. Assignments should be more fun to complete as you will not be anxious and stressed about meeting deadlines. Planning ahead helps you to know what you need to achieve and will help you to become more relaxed about your studies.

As we have seen in the previous chapter, mental and physical health is of utmost importance. If you want to maximize your productivity, keep your mind and body active, eat a healthy diet, get plenty of rest and avoid harmful substances (see Chapter 22). Also, take advantage of the wide variety of health, fitness and sporting facilities that are available to students in colleges and universities, some of which are free of charge.

Summary

As a student you will be able to study more successfully if you are well organized. You can do this through careful planning and by taking control of your time. A social life is very important to your well-being, but you need to make sure that it does not have a detrimental impact on your studies. If you have to work in paid employment you should seek advice about the recommended amount of hours you should work, and, again, make sure that it does not have an adverse influence on your studies. A healthy mind and body will help you to increase productivity.

These first two chapters have helped you to think about how you should prepare for your college or university study. The following chapters go on to look at specific study skills, starting with reading skills, which are discussed in the next chapter.

3 Enhancing your reading skills

Well-developed reading skills are vital to the success of your studies. The amount of reading that you will need to undertake depends on the subject you are studying, the level of your course, the preferences of your tutor and your personal interest and motivation.

To get the most out of your academic reading you need to make sure that you are well prepared, understand the reading process, improve your reading speed and know how to organize and record your reading. These issues are discussed in this chapter.

Preparing for academic reading

If you have not already done so, you should have your eyesight checked, as poor eyesight can affect your reading ability, development and learning. These tests also detect sight-threatening conditions at an early stage and underlying health conditions such as high blood pressure, diabetes, high cholesterol, increased risk of stroke and even tumours. You should have a test once every two years (or more often if recommended by your optician).

Tip Eye tests should be undertaken by a trained optician. Internet eye tests are no substitute for the real test.

According to the Eyecare Trust, 75% of British people are putting off having their sight tested due to concerns over the cost of eyecare, glasses and contact lenses. As a student you may feel that money is tight and that you cannot afford to have your eyes tested. However, you are entitled to free sight tests, paid for by the NHS, if you are under 16 years of age or you are 16, 17 or 18 and in full-time education (England, Wales and Northern Ireland). If you live in Scotland all eye tests are free.

Finding a place to read

In addition to having your eyes tested you need to work out where you are going to read. You need a quiet place, free from distractions, with good natural light during the day and good artificial light in the evenings. You will also need comfortable furniture.

Understanding the way we read

There are a number of ways in which we read, depending on our competence, purpose and type and level of reading required. When you begin to prepare for academic reading you need to be aware of the various ways that you read text. These include:

- recognizing letter sounds and the sounds of words;
- recognizing the meaning of words;
- understanding the sequence in which the words have been written;
- recognizing the look of words;
- predicting the order of the words;
- predicting the ideas contained within the words;
- skimming to get a general idea of what the text is about;

- skimming to recap what has been said;
- scanning to search for information to help predict;
- scanning to disregard irrelevant material;
- scanning for key words;
- understanding the meaning of the text;
- looking for meaning outside the context of the sentence;
- analysing what has been said and what has not been said;
- critiquing what you have read.

You will find that you use different reading methods for different types of reading (see exercise below). Once you begin to recognize how you read, you will be able to think about developing the methods that will help to improve your academic reading, such as recapping, disregarding, analysing, reviewing and critiquing.

Exercise

Choose a magazine article to read. Once you have finished the article, consult the above list and think about which of these methods you have used to read the text. Do the same with an online news report, thinking about what methods you have used to read the text.

After you have completed this task, choose a book from your reading list. Read the first chapter in the way that you would normally read a school/college/university book. Again, which methods have you used? Are they different from those you used for the article and report, or are they the same? Is there anything you need to think about more deeply in the academic text? Do you need to think about changing the way you read academic texts? If you do need to change the way you read, how are you going to do this?

Developing your academic reading

For successful reading to take place, the reading matter needs to be appropriate, relevant and suited to your individual style and interests. As a student you will not only be reading for meaning and accuracy, but you will also be reading for thought. What you read will help you to develop your own ideas about the subject. This means that your own personality, experiences and imagination are also involved in the reading process.

Reading actively

Reading is not passive but is an active process in which you draw from your own experiences, develop your own thoughts and learn to evaluate and critique the thoughts and ideas presented within the text. You can develop your academic reading skills and learn to read actively by considering the following points.

- Don't put off your reading. Begin as soon as you start the course, if not before.

- Learn how to use contents pages and indexes carefully. You will not have time to read every book from cover to cover, and on most courses this is not necessary. Think about the key issues or topics needed for your course or assignment and read sections of books that are relevant to these issues.

- Read introductions and summaries to find out whether the book or chapter is relevant.

- Take notes as you read, remembering to note down all sources that you use (see below).

- Set manageable sessions for your reading. With time you will begin to understand your own concentration levels.

Work within these levels. If you read for too long you will be unable to retain much of your reading or take in new information. Always have short breaks within your reading sessions to refresh your mind.

- Always keep your purpose in mind when reading.
- The more you read, the better you will become. Read as much as you can. Read around a subject, follow up interesting leads and make sure that you read all the recommended texts.

Improving reading speed

Some students feel that they read too slowly and that they won't have time to complete all the required reading. However, you should not let this put you off your reading. Instead, consider the following points.

- Reading speed improves with practice. The more you practise, the faster you will read.
- Reading speed improves with comprehension. As you become more familiar with your subject and the technical jargon used, you will find that you read faster. You will spend less time reviewing what you have read in an effort to understand the material.
- Reading speed improves with interest. If you are interested in what you are reading you will find that you read faster, especially when you are intrigued to know what happens next.
- Reading speed improves with motivation. If your motivation levels remain high, you will find it easier to read at a quicker pace and take in the material.

Reading too slowly

There are several reasons why people read slowly. It is not advisable to force yourself to read quicker without addressing these reasons as you may simply begin to read quicker but not improve your understanding of the material. Possible reasons for slow reading are outlined in the first column of Table 2. Suggestions for solving the problem and improving reading speed without losing comprehension are provided in the second column.

Table 2. Improving reading speed.

Reason for slow reading	Method for improving speed
The need to read the material word-by-word	Try to concentrate on key words and meaningful ideas rather than sounding out each word. Try to develop a wider eye-span that will help you to read more than one word at a time. This aids comprehension
Being slow to recognize and respond to material, usually due to technical jargon or difficult concepts and ideas	This will improve as you become more familiar with your subject. Talk through difficult ideas with other students or your tutor, or read another book that is easier to understand. If one sentence or paragraph is slowing you down, move on to the next. Sometimes the previous sentence becomes clearer as you progress
Problems with eyesight	Have your eyesight checked. Often slow reading is due to poor eyesight that has not been corrected (see above)
Problems with eye movements	Faulty eye movements can lead to problems with finding your place on the page, which will slow down your reading. A visit to your optician could solve the problem

Reason for slow reading	**Method for improving speed**
Lack of concentration	Read at a time when you are most productive, not when you are tired. Break reading sessions down into small, manageable chunks. Get plenty of sleep and keep active
Distractions	Find a quiet place to read, free from distractions. Notice when you are distracted from reading, and learn how to pull your mind back to the task. Make sure that other people understand that you are not to be disturbed
Lack of practice	Practise as much as possible. Many students find that this is the most effective way to improve reading speed and comprehension
Habitual slow reading	If you have always read slowly, it can be difficult to change, but it is possible. Begin by taking a simple text and force yourself to read quicker, without losing meaning. Gradually practise with more complex texts. Be aware of your reading rate and notice when you revert to slower reading
Re-reading the material	If you read slowly you may find that you have to re-read material to take it in. However, try not to do this as most ideas will be repeated again in the text. As your reading speed improves, you will find less need to re-read
Trying to remember everything	Consider what is important and remember facts selectively. This could be helped by writing a list of important issues prior to beginning reading
Dyslexia	If you have been diagnosed with dyslexia, or you think you might be dyslexic, find out what support is offered by your learning provider (see Appendix 2)

Adjusting your reading rate

Although it is desirable to increase your reading speed, to be successful in your studies you will need to know when to adjust your rate. For example, you will need to slow your rate when you encounter:

- ideas that need retaining;
- facts and figures that need to be committed to memory;
- unfamiliar terminology that needs exploring;
- difficult sentence or paragraph construction that needs unpicking;
- detailed technical instruction that needs clear understanding;
- unfamiliar or abstract concepts that need extra attention.

On the other hand, you can increase the speed of your reading when you encounter:

- irrelevant case studies, examples, illustrations or tables;
- material with which you are familiar and are being told nothing new;
- broad generalizations of ideas that have been stated previously;
- too much detail or elaboration that is unnecessary to your purpose.

Improving understanding

Try to understand and evaluate what you are reading. Don't read page after page without understanding the material. If you don't understand a text, discuss it with other students or with your tutor, or try another source of information that might explain the concepts in a better way.

Tip Don't ignore books aimed at someone younger or at the layperson. These books can often help to explain complex issues in a way that you can understand. You can move on to more complex texts once you have grasped the general idea.

You can improve your understanding of reading material by writing a list of what you need to find out before you begin reading. You should also include a list of questions that need answering. This will help you to focus your reading and stop you becoming distracted by irrelevant material (this is of particular importance when surfing the net for information).

When you've finished reading a section, think about whether there are any questions that remain unanswered. You can then return to the text, or to another source, to answer your questions.

Steps to aid understanding when reading

1. Make a list of what you want to find out, including questions that need answering.

2. Find the most relevant texts/sources of information.

3. Highlight the most important points as you read.

4. Record main headings as you read.

5. Write a few keywords under each heading.

6. Write a list of questions that form as you read.

7. Take note of the questions asked by the author.

8. Record answers to questions.

9. Summarize what you have read.

10. Re-read the text to check on the accuracy of your personal summary.

11. Return to the text, or other sources, if questions remain unanswered.

Organizing and recording your reading

It is important to be organized from the start of your course. You may find that you read a book or web page early in your course that becomes relevant later on, but if you haven't taken note of the book or web page, and the location, you may find it hard to find the source again (see quotation below). Therefore, you need to keep an accurate record of all reading from the beginning of your course.

> 'In my first year I read something about cash crops in West Africa and I'd really enjoyed it but because it wasn't related to an assignment I didn't take any notes. But it was something I was interested in, so when it came to my dissertation I decided that would be my subject. But when I went back to the library, could I find the book?
>
> It was really annoying because it had been a good book with a different political perspective. But I just couldn't find it. My tutor didn't know what it was either. I never did find it. What a shame. I do wish I'd kept a record.'
>
> Anna, University of Wolverhampton

Start organizing your notes immediately. Don't leave this until you have taken pages and pages of notes as they will be harder to organize. Remember to write down the bibliographical details of every relevant book/journal/website you read, and always note page numbers of relevant pieces or quotations that you intend to use in your assignments. Comprehensive information about how to organize notes and record bibliographical details is provided in Chapter 6.

Summary

All students need to develop their reading skills if they are to succeed on their course. Although most students find that their reading skills develop as their course progresses, there is other action that you can take to improve and develop your academic reading skills. This includes having your eyes checked, understanding how you read, improving reading speed, improving understanding and using library and online sources to their full potential.

Through developing your reading skills you will find that comprehension increases and your coursework becomes easier. You will also find that, through reading, you are able to improve your vocabulary, spelling, punctuation and grammar. These are skills that are essential to successful writing and are discussed in the next chapter.

4 Improving your English language skills

Good English language skills are extremely important for any college or university course that requires the submission of written work. Although some students struggle with the English language, especially if it is not their first language, it is possible to improve these skills with practice, patience, knowledge and perseverance. This chapter offers advice on improving your English language skills.

Improving your spelling

Spelling is a skill that you learn by reading and writing. It is also a visual skill that will improve with practice. Some English words can be hard to spell because many of them don't follow a regular pattern. Therefore, as a student, it is important to buy a good dictionary. This will help you with the spelling, the meaning and the proper use of the word.

The more you use a dictionary, the more your spelling will improve. Don't rely on the spell-check facility on your PC/laptop as it will pick up some words that have been spelt incorrectly, but will miss many others and won't aid your comprehension of the word.

'I write difficult words or technical words onto index cards and I carry them around with me. I write the word on one side of the card and the meaning on the other. I can check the cards on the bus,

when I'm having coffee or even walking to college. This helps me to spell the word and know the meaning of the word which is really important with some words, like epistemology!'

Suzanne, Bournemouth University

Overcoming problems with spelling

The following points address common problems faced by students. However, these are general rules and most do have exceptions. If in doubt about any spelling, consult your dictionary.

- Perhaps the most famous rule is to put 'i before e, except after c'. The exceptions to this rule include words such as forfeit, weird, neighbour and either.

- For many short words you double the last letter when you add an ending to them, e.g. omitted, fatter, biggest, dropping. Exceptions to this rule include buses, gases and entering.

- If a word ends with a silent 'e', when you are adding anything to the word you drop the 'e', e.g. caring, shining and conceivable. However, you keep the 'e' when there is a soft-sounding 'ce' or 'ge' ending, e.g. changeable and noticeable.

- Short words that end in 'll' have one of the 'l's dropped when you add to the words, e.g. handful, welcome and until. Exceptions to this rule include farewell, illness and tallness.

- Adjectives with one 'l' usually take a double 'll' when they become adverbs, e.g. real/really, careful/carefully.

- Verbs ending in 'ie' drop the 'e' when adding 'ing' or 'ed', e.g. lie/lying/lied. Notice also that the 'i' changes to a 'y' because you can't have two 'i's together.

- If a word ends in a double consonant and you add an ending, it is usual to retain both consonants, e.g. assess/assessment.

- When you add 'ness' to a word that ends in 'n' it is usual to keep both letter 'n's, e.g. keen/keenness.

- When a word ends in 'oe' you keep the letter 'e' when adding to the word, e.g. hoe/hoeing. However, if your addition begins with 'e' you will drop the 'e', e.g. hoe/hoed.

- When adding an extra part to a word, both consonants are retained so you have a double consonant within the words, e.g. unnecessary (un + necessary), withhold (with + hold).

Steps for improving spelling

1. Write the word down and study it carefully.

2. Say the word out loud.

3. Pronounce the word phonetically, each syllable at a time.

4. Cover up the word and try to spell it.

5. Check that the word is correct.

6. Repeat this process until you know the word.

7. Wait for a few days and then try to spell the word again.

8. Check that the word has been spelt correctly. If not, repeat the above process.

9. When you next encounter the word, pronounce it phonetically when you spell it.

Knowing how to punctuate

Punctuation is used to help the writer get their message across in a clear and concise manner. When we speak we make the

meaning clear by pausing, expressing words in different ways and adding facial and hand gestures. We cannot do this in writing, so instead we use punctuation to get across our meaning.

Although is not possible to discuss all aspects of punctuation within this book, the following points help to address the most common problems faced by students.

Capital letters

There are seven rules to follow when using capital letters.

- You always start a sentence with a capital letter.
- The pronoun 'I' is always written as a capital letter.
- Proper nouns, such as names of people and names of places, begin with a capital letter.
- Capital letters are used to begin the first word and the other main words in the title of a book, e.g. *The Complete Guide to Study Skills.*
- When you are referring to a particular month or a particular day of the week, you use a capital letter. However, you don't use a capital letter if you are referring to them in a general way, e.g. I don't like monday mornings.
- Capital letters are used at the beginning of a passage of direct speech, even if it is not the beginning of a sentence, e.g. she said, 'When will he arrive?'
- Capital letters are used in abbreviations only if capital letters are used for the full word or title, e.g. the Royal Society for the Prevention of Cruelty to Animals: RSPCA.

The comma

Commas indicate the shortest pause in a sentence. They can be used in six different ways.

- They can divide the items in a list, although a comma is not used to divide the last two words if they are separated by 'and', e.g. carpets, curtains, lamp shades and furniture.

- They are used to separate two or more adjectives connected to a noun, e.g. she was a shy, modest woman.

- If you want to insert an extra phrase into a sentence, you separate it from the main sentence by using commas, e.g. focus groups, although criticized by some people, are a useful method of data collection.

- If you use the adverbs 'however', 'therefore' or 'nevertheless' in mid-sentence you surround these by commas, e.g. focus groups, therefore, were the best method to use in this research.

- If you wish to add a phrase onto your main sentence you use a comma to separate the phrase, e.g. she decided to use focus groups in her research, even though she had no experience of the data collection technique.

- Direct speech is preceded by a comma, e.g. she said, 'I will enjoy using focus groups.'

The semicolon

The semicolon indicates a pause slightly longer than a comma. It is used in three ways.

- The semicolon should be used when dividing the items of a list when additional information about each item is supplied, e.g. carpets, which were red; curtains that had faded

in the light; lamp shades too numerous to mention and various items of furniture.

- Semicolons can be used to join two closely connected sentences, e.g. the focus group ran smoothly; she had been a good facilitator.

- Semicolons can be used in front of an adverb to indicate a slightly longer pause than a comma, e.g. the focus group finished after two hours of intensive discussion; so she was happy and went home.

The colon

The colon indicates a slightly longer pause than the semicolon but a slightly shorter pause than a full stop. Colons are used:

- to indicate the start of a list;
- to indicate the start of a long quotation;
- to introduce an explanation or elaboration of what has come before.

Brackets

Brackets are useful punctuation marks for students. They are used in three main ways.

- To reference a piece of material in your written text, e.g. (Dawson, 2003: 34).

- To add an extra piece of information to your sentence, e.g. the course fees are £2,300 (inclusive of field trips and materials).

- To add information after a person's name, e.g. Thomas Hardy (author).

The apostrophe

Apostrophes are one of the punctuation marks that students often get wrong. The most common mistake is that they are used when they are not needed. In fact, they are used only in two ways.

- To show where one or more letters have been missed out, e.g. it's (it is), don't (do not) and can't (cannot).

- To show ownership, e.g. my mother's books (the books of my mother). In this example the books belong to one person so the apostrophe is written before the 's'. However, if the books belong to several people, the apostrophe appears after the 's' to denote ownership, e.g. our mothers' books (the books of our mothers).

The dash

The dash is used to lengthen the pause between words and can be used in two main ways.

- It can be used instead of commas or brackets when you want to insert extra information into a sentence, e.g. the focus group was attended by eight people – three men and five women – and was a complete success.

- You can use it in the middle of a sentence when you wish to change the thought or idea being expressed, but don't want a full stop, e.g. I found essays really hard going – but that has improved now.

The hyphen

A hyphen is used to shorten the pause between words. It can be used in four main ways.

- To link two or more words together to form a word that has a different meaning, e.g. daughter-in-law, well-known, worth-while.

- To link prefixes, e.g. pre-war, ex-champion.

- To show that vowels are pronounced separately, e.g. co-operative.

- To make the meaning of a sentence become clearer, e.g. we expect you to attend for two hour-long lectures.

Exercise

When you have completed a written assignment, pretend that you are a tutor marking your work. Read through this chapter and 'mark' your assignment, noting any mistakes that you have made in light of what you have read in this chapter. This will help you to spot mistakes when you edit and proofread future assignments.

Developing your grammatical skills

'Grammar' is the term that is used to describe all the various things that make up the rules of language. If you hope to write well, you must pay close attention to these grammatical rules. Grammar is used in writing to help you get across your meaning, and make your writing interesting and engaging. Good grammar will also help to improve your marks.

It is not possible to cover the vast subject of English grammar within this book, so some useful sources of information and advice are provided at the end of this chapter for those of you who are struggling with your grammar. However, there are some common pitfalls that you should avoid, as detailed below.

Tense consistency

A common mistake is to change tense in the middle of a sentence or paragraph. When you are writing, choose an appropriate tense and stick to it. For example, when you are describing a chronological sequence of events you will find it useful to use the past tense, whereas when reviewing or critiquing an article or book the present tense may be more appropriate. Whichever you choose, make sure that it remains the same.

Split infinitives

The 'infinitive' of a verb is the form given in the dictionary where no specific subject is indicated, and it is characterized by the word 'to'. For example, to go, to see, to hear, to write, etc. A split infinitive is where another word is inserted into the infinitive. Examples include 'to madly run' and 'to quickly walk'. Change the order of the words to rectify the problem, e.g. 'he decided to run madly' and 'she wanted to walk quickly'.

> Perhaps the most common split infinitive was used at the beginning of *Star Trek*, where the mission of the *Enterprise* and her crew was 'to boldly go where no man has gone before'. This statement managed to upset both grammarians and feminists.

Run-on sentences

When you are writing it is easy to get carried away with a thought or idea. In some cases you may find that one sentence runs on into another as you try to get your ideas down onto paper. Run-on sentences are grammatically incorrect and you will lose marks if you do this.

When you edit and proofread your written work (see Chapter 5) check that you have not done this. If you have, split the sentence into two, or use commas, colons or semicolons to make your meaning clear (see above).

Improving your vocabulary

Your vocabulary will increase as you read, write and use your dictionary. In addition, you can increase your vocabulary further by considering the following points.

- When you encounter a new word in your lectures or classes, write it down and look up the word after your lecture has finished. You might find it useful to keep a separate notebook that contains definitions of new words.

- If you encounter new words during your reading, make a note of the word and use your dictionary or the 'glossary of terms' to find its meaning. If the word is crucial to understand the meaning of what you are reading, you will need to do this straightaway. However, it is usually better not to disrupt your reading, but to look up all words that you don't understand when you have finished.

- Read as much as you can.

- Try to use any new words you have learned in your speech or writing.

Tip   Don't be afraid to ask tutors what a word means. Other students probably don't know the meaning but are too afraid to ask.

Seeking and receiving help

If you know that you have a problem with your English language skills you should seek help from your college or university. Most run additional classes and/or study sessions for people who are struggling. Some of these are aimed at people who speak English as their second language and others are aimed at English speakers who require additional help and support.

Speak to your tutor or contact your university international office for advice about what is available. More information about study skills support is provided in Appendix 2.

Taking note of tutor feedback

When your tutors marks your work they will correct your spelling, punctuation and grammar, or they will point out the problems and expect you to rectify them. Look very carefully at what they have highlighted. Understand where you have made a mistake and learn from your mistakes in future assignments.

If you don't understand where you have gone wrong, ask your tutor for clarification. You may also find it useful to ask another student to look at your assignment before it is handed in, and you can do the same for them (see quotation below).

'Me and my mate Alice go over each other's work before we give it to him [the tutor]. It does help, yeah, you know, 'cos I can see what's wrong with hers and she can see what's wrong with mine…I don't mind when she says, you know, you idiot, you've done that wrong …it helps and she don't mind either, but yeah, you know, you've got to be good friends, like.'

Amy, Weymouth College

Summary

Although some students struggle with spelling, punctuation, grammar and vocabulary, these are skills that will improve through practice and perseverance. The more you read and write, the more you will improve. However, it is important that you are active in the learning process and that you take on board feedback from your tutor and seek additional help, if required.

Improving your English language skills is only one part of producing good assignments. In addition, you will need to make sure that your work is well structured, pitched at the correct level and well argued. These issues are discussed in the following chapter.

Further information

www.bbc.co.uk/skillswise/words/grammar

Visit these pages of the BBC website for information, advice, tips and exercises that will help you to improve your grammar. They include information about adverbs, apostrophes, personal pronouns, using commas, making sentences, getting the right tense and avoiding double negatives.

www.bbc.co.uk/skillswise/words/spelling

Visit these pages of the BBC website for information, advice, tips and exercises that will help you to improve your spelling. They include information about root words, suffixes, words that sound the same, confusing words, letter patterns and spelling plurals.

Further reading

Leech, G. et al., *An A-Z of English Grammar and Usage* (Harlow: Pearson Education Limited, 2009).

5 Enhancing your writing skills

Good writing skills are crucial to successful study. University courses and higher-level college courses require you to submit both long and short assignments that must be well presented, well structured and well argued. They must also be grammatically correct (see Chapter 4).

Writing is a skill that can be learned and your writing ability will improve with increased knowledge and practice. This chapter provides advice and information on how to improve your writing skills for school, college and university courses.

Writing at the correct level and pitch

To find out how to write at the correct level and pitch, ask your tutor to provide examples of successful assignments completed by previous students on the course. Read through the assignments and ask the following questions.

1. How has the assignment been written?
2. What information has been included?
3. How has the author structured their argument?
4. What technical jargon has been used?
5. How much knowledge of the subject does the reader require to be able to understand the writing?
6. Do you understand what has been written?

Some tutors, however, may prefer not to provide examples of other work because they believe this stifles your creativity. If this is the case, write a draft assignment and discuss it thoroughly with your tutor, who will be able to give you positive and constructive feedback for your final version.

Developing a concise writing style

On most courses you will be required to complete your assignments within a specified amount of words. Don't be tempted to produce more than the maximum amount of words in the hope that you will receive more marks, because this will not be the case. Indeed, some tutors will penalize you heavily for exceeding the maximum word count.

To produce successful assignments you will need to cultivate a concise writing style that will enable you to pack as many ideas and arguments into your assignment as possible. The following tips will help you to do this.

- Keep the audience and purpose of your work in mind.

- Prioritize the main points. Go through your list to ensure that all points are relevant before you begin to write.

- Keep sentences short and make sure that your paragraphs are not too long.

- Only use quotations if they are relevant and help to explain a point you are trying to make.

- Don't include irrelevant material, however interesting. Stick to the question. When you read a draft version of your assignment, make sure that every part of your writing is relevant and delete if not. Your marks will improve if you are able to show that you can discriminate between relevant and irrelevant information (see over).

Tip In mathematics and science subjects, don't use words when a table or diagram would better illustrate the point that you are trying to make.

Structuring essays and assignments

You will find it easier to structure essays and assignments if you break the task down into the stages outlined below.

Stage 1: Choose a topic

On some courses you will be given only one topic, in which case the choice is already made for you. If, however, you are presented with a list of topics, you must decide which you wish to discuss.

When choosing a topic don't waste too much time making your decision. Look at each topic in turn and jot down a few points about each. This will give you an indication about your current knowledge, what interests you and the topics that you know nothing about.

Stage 2: Understand what is being asked

If you have to answer a specific question, make sure that you understand what is being asked. You might find it useful to discuss the question with other students to make sure that you have interpreted it correctly. If you are really unsure, arrange a meeting with your tutor to discuss the question in more depth.

Stage 3: Identify key areas

Once you have chosen your topic and/or understood the question, identify a number of key areas that will help direct your background reading. These key areas could change as your reading progresses, but your initial list will help you to identify important sources of information.

Stage 4: Begin your reading

In the early stages of your reading you may find it useful to identify a general, user-friendly text that helps you to consider the overall question and topic. This will enable you to develop ideas for more in-depth reading (see Chapter 3).

Stage 5: Take notes

Start to take notes as soon as you begin reading. Write down the main points and issues that relate to the question/topic. Collect facts and opinions. Record all sources you use, noting down the page numbers of any quotations that you intend to use (see Chapter 6).

Stage 6: Follow-up reading

As your reading progresses you should get a feel for what is relevant reading matter. This will help you to follow up your general reading with specialist reading (e.g. journal articles and conference papers). Use the bibliographies of books that you have found useful to steer you in specialist directions.

When you write your assignment you should include information from a variety of sources as this will show that you have covered the topic comprehensively.

Stage 7: Develop arguments

As you read you will find that ideas and arguments are forming about the topic. Note these down as soon as they form. You can then return to the reading to find evidence to support your arguments.

Stage 8: Begin to develop your main argument

Your main argument will develop with further reading. Take a little time to work through this argument, finding evidence from your notes to support your ideas. You may decide that you have enough information available, or you may feel that you need to return to your reading for more evidence.

Stage 9: Return to the question

Once you have developed your main argument, return to the question to check that you are working within the topic and have not got sidetracked with irrelevant information.

Stage 10: Organize your notes and arguments

Once you are happy that your main argument is relevant, you can begin to organize your notes and arguments into a coherent, logical structure. At this stage you should think about the order in which information should be presented in your assignment.

Stage 11: Write a draft introduction

Your introduction needs to begin with a general statement and should do the following:

- identify the key points in relation to the topic;
- provide a brief answer to the question, or a summary of your argument;
- provide a plan or a guide as to how the question will be answered.

Tip Some people find the introduction the hardest part to write. If this is the case, you may find it easier to write the introduction after you have written a draft main section and conclusion.

Stage 12: Write a draft main section

This section should follow the points set out in the introduction. It should contain your argument backed up by evidence for each point you discuss. Any evidence you use should be well referenced (see Chapters 6 and 18). Use transition sentences to move from one paragraph or one argument to the next. This can be done by repeating key ideas and words.

Stage 13: Write a draft conclusion

This should sum up your argument and leave the reader in no doubt as to the answer to the question and/or your view on the topic. Your assignment should finish with a clear, succinct statement.

Tip Write down several sentences that sum up your main argument. Choose the best for your conclusion.

Stage 14: Produce the references and bibliography

The reference section includes all the literature to which you have referred in your assignment. If you have read other publications but not referred to them when writing your assignment, you should include them as a bibliography at the end of your assignment (see Chapter 18). You will find this task easier to complete if you keep meticulous notes (see Chapter 6).

Stage 15: Review the draft

Read through your draft assignment, picking up on any weak points in your argument and any problems you have with structure. You may find that you have to return to your reading if you have missed any important points.

Stage 16: Redraft your assignment

Rewrite your assignment, altering the structure and content if required and checking that all references are clear. Make sure that your assignment is within the required word or page limit.

> 'I was really scared about doing my first university assignment 'cos I thought I just wasn't clever enough. But I wrote a draft and then I asked my husband to read it. He pointed out some problems and I rewrote it. Then I asked a good friend to look at it. She did the same and I rewrote it again. I was really nervous waiting for the marks, but I got 82%. I couldn't believe it. For my first assignment I got that much. It was a great confidence boost.'
>
> Jennifer, Open University

Editing and proofreading

Once you are happy with your draft assignment in terms of content and structure, you need to go through your work checking for grammatical errors and spelling mistakes (see Chapter 4). Don't rely on software to do this as some mistakes will be missed and automatic changes can be wrong.

Tip   When proofreading, read each word individually as it will help you to spot mistakes. Slow down your reading. When you read quickly you assume the word is right and will see it on the page as right, even if it is not. Also, read your assignment out loud. Hearing your words will help you to determine whether your writing flows well.

Some students find it useful to leave their work for a couple of days, if they have time, and then proofread. This is because they can approach the work with a fresh mind and spot mistakes that they have missed previously.

Others find it useful to work with a friend and proofread each other's assignment. Often it can be easier to detect mistakes in someone else's work.

Tips for improving marks

Present your work neatly.

Make sure there are no grammatical, spelling or typing mistakes.

Use good quality paper and make sure that there is plenty of toner/ink in your printer.

Avoid long, complex sentences and terminology that you don't understand.

Your introduction should flow nicely into the main section and on into the conclusion.

Present all arguments in a concise, well-reasoned way.

Keep ideas together that belong together.

Don't change ideas or arguments mid-paragraph.

Back up all your arguments with relevant evidence.

Reproduce and reference all quotations carefully.

Avoid plagiarism (using the thoughts, words and arguments of others).

Answer the question and keep your work free from irrelevant material.

Produce a draft, rewrite and then rewrite again.

Keep to the required length.

Hand in your work on time.

Overcoming writer's block

Even the most accomplished writers suffer from writer's block. However, there is action that you can take to overcome problems.

- Get up and move around if it helps your ideas to flow.
- Move to a different place where you might find it easier to write.
- Have a break and return to your work when you feel refreshed.
- Divide your work into short periods.
- Brainstorm each section of your assignment as a list and return to it when you feel comfortable writing.
- Use mind-maps, index cards or record your voice to get your ideas flowing.
- Discuss your ideas with a friend or relative.
- Don't be afraid to write in the wrong order. If you are struggling with one part of your assignment, move on to something else.
- Put together your bibliography or references if you are unable to write any other section of your assignment.
- Write a draft, however bad. You can rewrite at a later stage.

Summary

Good writing skills are essential for students, especially for those who need to complete written assignments, projects and dissertations. Writing is not a talent reserved for a select few, but is a skill that can be learned. Ask your tutor, read books and write as much as possible. To be able to write well you need to know how to write your assignment at the correct level, structure your arguments and back them up with relevant evidence. All work should be neatly presented.

An important part of being able to write successful essays and assignments is to understand how to take notes effectively and efficiently. These issues are discussed in the following chapter.

Further reading

Hennessy, B., *Writing an Essay: Simple techniques to transform your coursework and examinations*, 5th edition (Oxford: How To Books, 2007).

Weyers, J. and McMillan, K., *How to Write Essays and Assignments* (Harlow: Pearson Education, 2009).

6 Taking effective notes

If you want to make the most of your reading and be able to write well, you need to take notes effectively. This includes taking notes from books, journals and online sources, taking notes in class, using online note-taking applications, knowing how to organize your notes and understanding issues of plagiarism and copyright. These issues are discussed in this chapter.

Taking notes from books and journals

When you begin to take notes, think about the following points.

- Make notes that will aid your understanding and help you to review and revise what you have read.

- Don't copy chunks of text from the book or journal. Read the relevant sections, think about what you have read and make a few brief notes written in your own words. This will aid understanding and ensure that you are not using the sentences of others in your written work (see plagiarism on page 64).

- If you come across a useful quotation, write it down exactly, word-for-word. Check that you have copied it correctly if you intend to use it in an assignment. In your notes, write 'quotation' in the margin, or use quotation marks so that you are clear that it is a quotation. Take note of all the required bibliographical details (see below).

▓ Organize your notes as soon as you start taking them (see page 62).

Noting references and bibliographical details

When you have read a relevant text, take careful bibliographical details of what you have read. This will help you to find the source again, if you need to, and will enable you to include all the relevant information in the reference section and bibliography of your essays, assignments, projects and dissertations.

Tip Use the correct referencing procedure as soon as your course begins so that you can develop good habits from the start.

Books

Bibliographical details for books should include:

▓ author's surname and initials;

▓ date of publication;

▓ book title;

▓ publisher;

▓ place of publication;

▓ page numbers of specific information or quotations.

Journals

Bibliographical details for journals should include:

▓ author's surname and initials;

▓ article title;

▓ journal title;

▓ volume and/or number of the journal.

▓ page numbers of the article within the journal.

Tip Remember to note all bibliographical details at the time of accessing the information as it can be very difficult and time-consuming to retrace your reading at a later date.

Taking notes from online sources

When you take notes from online sources you should adopt a similar procedure to the method used for books and journals, described above. You may also find it useful to use online note-taking applications to store, organize and search through your notes (see next page).

Cutting and pasting information

Although it is tempting to cut and paste information from relevant websites, you must be careful if you choose to adopt this procedure. All cut-and-paste sections must be clearly marked so that you don't accidentally (or intentionally) pass off the information as your own work. This is plagiarism and it is a serious offence. Universities may use plagiarism-detection software to catch students who cheat in this way.

However, it is possible to cut and paste relevant quotations, as long as you use quotation marks in your report and reference the work carefully and correctly. For more information about plagiarism, see page 64.

Noting online references and bibliographical details

You must make sure that you record all online reference and bibliographical information at the time that you access a website. This is because, first, you may find it very difficult to find the information at a later date and, second, websites and the information contained within them change frequently.

At this present time the way you are asked to reference material from the internet varies, so speak to your tutor about what information is required. In general, you will need to note the following:

- author's surname and initials (if known);
- date of publication or last revision;
- title of document;
- title of complete work (if relevant);
- URL/web address;
- date of access.

Tip If you decide to store bibliographical information electronically, it is a simple job to cut and paste your references when you come to compile the reference section and bibliography of your report, assignment or dissertation.

Using online note-taking applications

There are a wide variety of online note-taking tools available. These enable you to:

- save whole web pages or small snippets of information found while conducting online research;

▨ save images and links;

▨ organize your notes;

▨ search your notes;

▨ store lecture/seminar notes;

▨ share your notes with other students;

▨ collaborate with others in group or project work.

These note-taking applications can be useful for students, for example, if you have missed a lecture, or if you don't understand something that has been said. You can share your notes with each other, add to the notes and learn from each other. To find out what is available, enter 'free note-taking applications' into your search engine, or speak to your tutor/IT technician at college or university.

Taking notes in lectures and seminars

Some students use an A4 lined writing pad to take notes in lectures and seminars, whereas others use laptops. The choice is yours (unless your institution or tutor forbids the use of laptops – see quotation below). Find the method that suits you best. You may need to try each for a few weeks and then decide which is the most effective for you, personally.

> 'Although our campus is now wireless and most new students have laptops I decided to forbid them in my classes. This is because when students use a laptop to take notes they tend to take a verbatim transcription. Their eyes glaze over and they don't seem to be part of my class. They also can't contribute to the discussion.
>
> When students take notes by hand it is a much slower process and they have to listen to what I say and process the information while they are taking notes.

I did some informal research with my students and they actually said that they find it better without laptops because they listen more and are more engaged. Some even admitted to doing other things, such as checking email, when they were in class. This is distracting for them but also distracts others around them.'

David, lecturer in research methods

Improving your note-taking skills

You can improve your note-taking skills in lectures and classes by considering the following points.

■ Don't try to write down everything you hear (this is of particular importance if using a laptop – see quotation above). Instead, listen for the main points and make sure that these are included in your notes. However, in maths and science subjects you might need to copy everything the lecturer writes on the board verbatim, as every symbol means something specific.

■ Most people have to stop listening to write, so be selective about when you decide to write so that you don't miss any salient points.

■ Use diagrams, if appropriate, to aid understanding.

■ Leave wide margins on either side of your notes if using A4 paper. This means that you can add extra information if the tutor returns to a previous point and when you review your notes after the lecture.

■ Use question marks to query any information that you don't understand and to which you may need to return at a later date.

■ Visual aids are used by lecturers to emphasize a point. Analyse carefully what you are being shown and take relevant notes, leaving spaces so that you can fill in the gaps when you review your notes.

▧ If you are listening actively you will find that questions are forming in your mind (see Chapter 7). Jot down these questions. You can ask your tutor for clarification at a later stage, or search for the answer from a different source.

Organizing your paper notes

Keep your paper notes well organized as you will find it easier to obtain material for assignments and to revise for examinations. When you attend a lecture or seminar write the subject, date, course code, name of lecturer and topic to be discussed at the top of the page and make sure that you begin each lecture with a new page.

Summarize the main points of the lecture/seminar and include these with your notes. File your notes and summaries together with topics that cover the same or related areas. Have one A4 ring-binder file for each subject/module.

Reviewing your notes

After each lecture or seminar it is important to review and organize your notes as this helps you to retain information. Also, you may find that some of your notes are disorganized and need rewriting so that you can make sense of them. It is best to review and organize your notes as soon as possible after the lecture or seminar when the information is fresh in your mind.

Follow up the lecture or seminar with additional reading that will help to clarify points. File your background reading notes with your lecture/seminar notes, if they are on the same topic. Include numbers and labels on pages so that you can keep them in the right order.

Organizing your electronic notes

If you take notes using a laptop make sure that your notes are well organized. The method that you choose will be dictated by personal preference, but you need to ensure that you understand your system and can access information easily. Software is available to help you to organize your notes, but if you choose this method, make sure that you use software that is easy to understand and helps you to become more efficient.

A common method of organization is to have a separate document for each lecture, carefully labelled by date and topic. These can be placed in a folder for each subject/module. Keep document and folder names simple so that you can access the information easily when required (see quotation below). Remember to back up all folders and documents on a regular basis. Keep back-up copies in a separate place, away from your PC/laptop.

> 'When I did my access course I didn't really think too much about storing my files, you know, I didn't think about what to call them, then I had terrible trouble finding a file when I needed it...Yes, I make sure I'm very specific with what I call them so that I can find all my work very easily.'
>
> Alison, Sheffield Hallam University.

Reviewing your electronic notes

Again, you need to review your notes after each lecture to make sure that you have understood what has been said. You might find it useful to summarize the information into headings and key words, especially if you find that you have been tempted to take notes verbatim.

Understanding plagiarism

'Plagiarism' is the act of taking credit, or stealing, the words, ideas and arguments of others. You can use work by other people, but you must acknowledge your source and make it clear that you are using the work of others. The problem arises when work is not acknowledged and students try to pass it off as their own. Serious plagiarism can lead to assignment failure and even expulsion from your course.

All colleges and universities have strict rules about plagiarism. You can obtain a list of rules and regulations from your tutor or more information about plagiarism can be obtained from www.jisc.ac.uk.

Exercise

A useful way to make sure that you haven't accidentally plagiarized the words of others is to use one of the free plagiarism checkers now available on the internet. Enter 'free plagiarism checker' into your search engine and choose one that will enable you to cut and paste your whole essay/assignment into the search facility.

The checker will go through your work and detect whether your words are 'OK' or whether 'plagiarism is detected'. If the latter is the case, follow the link to the original source to find out whether you have accidentally plagiarized. If so, you will need to rewrite that section of your work or acknowledge the source.

Understanding copyright

There are some advantages to taking photocopies instead of notes, for example, that:

- it is quicker to photocopy articles than take notes;

- you are able to highlight salient points on the actual photocopy;

- it is useful if some books are in short supply or are reference only, and cannot be taken from the library.

However, if you decide to photocopy any material you must do so within copyright law. This states that you cannot photocopy more than one chapter of a book or one article of a journal, and that what you photocopy cannot be more than 5% of the work. More information about copyright can be obtained from the Copyright Licensing Agency: www.cla. co.uk.

Summary

As a student you will be required to take notes from books, journals and online sources, and in class. It is important to be organized when taking notes. You need to make sure that you keep careful records and bibliographical details so that you can return to sources if required and so that you can reference correctly and accurately. Software is available to help you to do this. You also need to understand issues of plagiarism and copyright when taking notes.

You cannot take effective notes in class without knowing how to listen properly to what you are being told. These issues are discussed in the following chapter.

7 Improving your listening skills

Good listening skills are essential for students. If you listen well you will be able to take class notes more efficiently, groupwork will be more productive and research projects more successful. This chapter provides advice on becoming an effective listener in the different situations that you may encounter on your course.

Becoming an active listener

Active listening involves one person listening carefully to the words of another and understanding, evaluating and interpreting what they hear. To listen actively you need to be able to concentrate on what the speaker is saying and free your mind from distractions. Even if you don't agree with what is being said, you need to continue to listen rather than become distracted with the development of your own thoughts and arguments.

Understanding distractions

To become an active listener you need to understand what issues can distract you from listening. This could be external distractions, such as noises in the room or students talking among themselves, or internal distractions, such as allowing your mind to drift to other matters. More information about recognizing and overcoming learning distractions is provided in Chapter 1.

You may also be distracted by unfamiliar terminology, or a feeling of being overwhelmed by the subject matter. If this is the case, you will find it useful to follow the lecture preparation guidelines provided in Chapter 14 and the information about increasing your vocabulary, provided in Chapter 4.

Exercise

Listen to a radio talk show or a TV broadcast. Try to pay full attention to what you are hearing. If you find your mind drifting, take a note of what has distracted you. Repeat this exercise in your first few lectures/classes. Become aware of distractions and pull your mind back to what is being said. Once you have increased your awareness of what can distract you from listening, it will be easier to overcome listening problems in the future.

Improving your listening skills in lectures and classes

To get the most out of lectures and classes you need to prepare thoroughly (see Chapter 14). If you read around the subject before you attend, you will become familiar with some of the terms, concepts, ideas and arguments that will be presented. This will stop you from becoming distracted due to a lack of understanding, which will help you to listen more effectively and take better notes. You will also be able to note down any issues that need clarification at a later date.

Developing effective listening skills

The following points will help you to develop effective listening skills in lectures and classes.

- Listen for the main points. Most good tutors will introduce the session with these main points and then summarize them in their conclusion.

- Listen willingly. Enjoy the lecture/class and note all the interesting points that are being made.

- Listen for clues about material to include in examinations and assignments. You will find it easier to listen because you have a purpose for listening carefully and picking up on salient points. These clues may be given through what the tutor says and how they say it; for example, in their intonations, repetition, hand gestures and volume and pitch of voice.

- If there is a pause or break, summarize what you have learned so far. Note down any relevant questions that you need to answer at a later date.

- Try to hear what is being said, not what you want or expect to hear.

Effective listening in groupwork

For groups to work well, active listening has to be an activity undertaken by all members of the group. When the whole group is involved in active listening, groupwork runs much more smoothly and is free from individual annoyance or frustration.

You should be involved within the group, listening to other people, forming your own opinions and letting other people know what you think. Remember that other members of the group might be unconfident or nervous about speaking in a group setting. Give them chance to speak and make sure that you, and other members of the group, listen to what they have to say.

Exercise

We all know how frustrating it can be when we know that someone is not listening to us. But what are the clues that this is the case? Think of a situation during which you were sure that someone was not listening to you. List all the clues that suggested they were not listening. Then consult the list below to see whether you have picked up on similar points.

Non-listening clues

When I conducted this exercise with students, their list included:

- no eye contact;
- fidgeting, fiddling and/or doodling;
- interrupting what you are saying;
- finishing the sentence for you, even if they are wrong;
- saying something that has no relevance to what you have just said;
- misunderstanding/not hearing what you have said;
- walking away or turning away when you are in mid-sentence;
- continuing with their own ideas/arguments, with no recognition of your ideas and arguments.

Improving listening behaviour

Once you have noticed the clues that indicate someone is not listening to you, it is possible to improve your own listening behaviour. This will not only show that you are listening (and hence improve group morale and communication) but also help you to listen more effectively and get more out of the group.

Therefore, to listen to others you should consider the following.

- Always make eye contact with the speaker. This shows that you are interested in what they are saying.

- Try not to be distracted when someone is speaking. Don't fiddle with a pen, play with your laptop, look out the window or respond to others who are not speaking.

- When someone is speaking, take note of the words they are using and the ideas they are expressing. Start to distinguish between opinions, prejudice and fact.

- Make sure that you let someone finish speaking. Don't jump to conclusions about what they are going to say.

- Although it is acceptable to interrupt occasionally with a well thought-out question or opinion, don't do it too often or in a confrontational way as this will cause ill-feeling and may lead to other members of the group becoming defensive.

- If you are unsure of what someone is saying, ask questions. Try to ask open questions that start with words such as 'what', 'why', 'where' and 'how' as people cannot answer these with a simple yes or no and will have to elaborate on what they are saying.

> **Tip** If you agree with what someone has said, express your support and opinion. We all like to receive encouragement from others, especially if we are nervous or slightly unsure of what we are saying.

Listening to tutor feedback

Although you may think of your tutor as an instructor or conveyor of knowledge, you should also think of them as a partner in the learning process. Studying and learning are interactive processes and should be seen as part of a conversation that takes place between scholar and student. Therefore, any feedback your tutor gives should be listened to carefully and you should act on their advice.

> **Tip** All feedback is for your benefit, so make sure that you learn as much as you can from what is being said. If you don't understand something, ask for clarification.

Some tutors are better than others at providing constructive or positive feedback. Some may appear blunt or rude so don't take their comments personally, but try to take them for what they are (helpful pieces of advice on how your work can improve). Keep your emotions away from what you are being told. Learn from the comments and seek further advice or clarification, if required.

> **Tip** Don't mistake critical feedback for negative feedback. Your tutor is not interested in boosting your ego, but is interested in developing your academic abilities.

Receiving written feedback

On many courses you may not meet your tutor face-to-face, but instead will receive written feedback, either through the post or via e-mail. Make sure that you collect all assignments and take note of all feedback. It has been suggested that, on some courses, almost 40% of students don't collect their assignments. This is because they are interested only in receiving their marks and fail to realize that tutor feedback is essential to their academic development.

Listening to research participants

Good listening skills are essential if you intend to carry out research with other people. Some project work may require you to speak to others and many undergraduates will have to conduct social research for their dissertation (see Chapters 16, 17 and 18).

If you have to interview individuals or groups, you can improve your ability to listen by taking note of the following points.

- Choose a venue that is free from noisy distractions and interruptions.
- Sit close enough so that you can hear your participant(s), but don't invade their space.
- Make firm eye contact and don't fiddle or fidget. Show that you are listening properly as this will encourage people to open up.
- Don't be distracted by any audio devices that you are using (see next page).
- If you are unsure of what is being said, ask for clarification and probe for more information. You can only do this if you remain alert and listen to everything that is being said.

- Repeat the last few words that someone has said, turning it into a question. This shows that you are listening to what they are saying and that you are interested in their words. This encourages them to say more.

- Summarize what people have said as a way of finding out if you have listened carefully, understood what has been said and to determine whether they wish to add any further information.

Tip Don't be afraid of silences. Most people are uncomfortable during silences and will elaborate on what they've said rather than experience discomfort. This enables you to gather more information.

Using audio devices in research

If you choose to use audio devices when you interview people, it is important to remember that this is not a substitute for careful listening. You need to listen intently so that you can ask further questions and encourage a more in-depth response. As we have seen above, people are more likely to open up if they know that someone is listening to them and value what they are saying.

If you choose to use audio devices for your research, you should take note of the following.

- Check all equipment thoroughly beforehand and make sure that you know how it works.

- Place the equipment on a non-vibratory surface, close enough to the participant(s) so that every voice can be picked up. You will need to check this prior to the interview. Make sure that there are no outside noises that could disrupt your recording.

▦ Make sure that there is a clear battery indicator light on your equipment. This will enable you to check that it is still working without drawing attention to the machine (you don't want to do this because some people are self-conscious about being recorded, and it is better that they try to forget that the machine is there).

▦ Although you are recording, take a pen and notepad with you so that you can write down any questions and issues that you need to return to at a later time. However, only jot down a few points, and try to maintain eye contact for as long as possible while you are writing.

▦ Continue to concentrate and listen to what is being said. Don't become complacent because the interview is being recorded (see quotation below). The equipment could fail, or not work as well as you had intended, and you need to listen carefully to be able to probe for more information.

'It was my fourth interview of the day and I was whacked. That's too many in a day. It tires you…I thought it was all being recorded, 'cos I'd done loads before and never had any problems. I didn't write anything down 'cos I was tired and I'd had enough really… I couldn't believe it, none of it recorded. Nothing, it was all gone. And, 'cos I was tired I didn't check it 'till the next day. I should have checked immediately and written down as much as I could remember. But it was the next day and loads of interviews all merged into one. I couldn't remember it all.'

Sam, Sheffield Hallam University

Using audio devices in lectures and classes

Today, there are a variety of digital audio devices that can be used in classes, lectures and seminars, including MP3s with built-in microphones and recording facilities, and smart pens that enable you to record what you write and hear, and synchronize both. Whether you choose to use such technology is a personal choice and depends on your personal finances.

Possible benefits include the following.

- You can listen to the lecture several times to clarify points and dissect what you have heard.

- It is useful for people who may struggle with the English language or subject terminology. You can listen again until the words and terms become more familiar.

- You can listen again and fill in any gaps in your notes, perhaps where you were distracted during the lecture.

- You can listen again, with a higher volume, if you have hearing difficulties.

- A recording helps you to understand academics who may have a strong accent.

Tutors understand the importance of repetition, and being able to listen again, so many are now offering their lectures as podcasts. If these are provided on your course it negates the need to record the lecture yourself (see Chapter 13).

Summary

Good listening skills are vital to the success of your studies. As a student you need to become an active listener as this will help you to listen to, take in, evaluate, interpret and understand what you are being told. This could be during lectures and seminars, during groupwork or when you undertake research for your course. There is an increasing number of audio devices available that enable you to listen again to what has been said, although these should not be a substitute for good listening skills.

If you learn to listen well you will find that you are able to think about what is being said and begin to form your own ideas. In addition to active listening, there are other factors involved in developing your thinking skills. These are discussed in the following chapter.

8 Developing your thinking skills

It is important that, as a student, you learn how to develop your thinking skills. This will help you to ask questions about information you are receiving and enable you to critique and analyse the work of others. You will also be able to develop your own theories, recognize bias and understand issues of objectivity and subjectivity. These issues are discussed in this chapter.

Understanding how we think

There are a number of methods that we use to think about an issue and an awareness of these will help you to develop your own thinking skills.

- **Visualization**. This method involves the creation of a picture in our minds to help us to think about the issue. Or we may decide to draw a graph or a diagram that helps us to clarify our thoughts. Visualization can be a useful method to adopt for complex scientific problems, for example (see Chapter 10).

- **Brainstorming**. Using this method we think about an issue and write down any thought that comes to mind, without judgement or reflection. The goal is to come up with a list that can be returned to, discussed and analysed at a later date. Brainstorming can be a useful way to begin an assignment or a research project.

- **Critical thinking**. This involves making judgements about an issue, idea or concept. This type of thinking can be used when trying to understand, evaluate, analyse and develop your own arguments or critique the work of others.

- **Lateral thinking**. This involves approaching an issue through an indirect route that does not follow logical ways of thought. This method of thinking is useful if you want to create new ideas, perhaps for a unique project.

- **Logical thinking**. This way of thinking follows a logical, sequential order. This method is useful for solving complex mathematics problems, for example (see Chapter 11).

Tip All thinking takes place within a particular time and culture and can be influenced by power, privilege and trends. The essence of real critical thinking is to recognize that knowledge and thinking cannot be reduced to skills alone and that outside influences play their part.

Developing thoughts and imagination

You can develop your thoughts and imagination by trying the different ways of thinking discussed above. When you encounter an issue that you wish to think about more deeply, work through each of the methods to find out which works best. As we have seen in Chapter 1, we all learn in different ways and a method that works for one person may not work for another. You need to find the most effective method (or methods) that work for you, and then use them to develop further your thoughts and imagination.

You may find that the method you adopt depends on the issue that you wish to think about, as some methods are more suited to certain issues. For example, mathematical and scientific problems may require you to work through a logical sequence to find the answer, whereas a particular philosophical conundrum may require lateral thought.

> 'At the beginning of the course I encourage my students to try as many different ways of thinking as possible. It opens up their minds, especially some of those who've only been used to answering multiple choice questions. I'm always surprised by how creative they can become and the lessons are fun. We come up with some incredible pictures, maps and lists. I would encourage all students to try different ways as it opens up their minds.'
>
> Sheila, Weymouth College

Learning how to question

You can develop your thinking skills further by learning how to ask questions. Being able to ask the right questions is fundamental to your studies, not only when you conduct your own piece of research, but when you listen to lectures, read books and talk to other students. If you don't ask questions you can't deepen your thinking, reflect on what you are learning, query the arguments of others or develop your own ideas.

Exercise

Take note of the questions that your tutor asks in class. What are the questions designed to do? What happens when a question is asked? Do some questions work better than others? Jot down a list of what you perceive to be good and bad questions.

Recognizing good and bad questions

Once you have undertaken the exercise described above, you should be able to recognize the difference between good and bad questions. Examples of good, useful questions include:

- open questions that require more than one-word answers;
- questions that make you think;
- questions that stimulate reflection;
- relevant and 'real' questions that have meaning;
- questions that introduce a problem;
- questions that test existing assumptions.

Examples of bad questions include:

- trick questions;
- sterile questions that constrain thought;
- questions that are too simple, irrelevant or patronizing;
- questions for which the answer is readily available;
- closed questions that require only one-word answers.

Solving problems

In addition to asking questions, solving problems will help you to develop your thinking skills further. A problem exists when you are curious, puzzled, confused or not sure how to resolve an issue. There are different ways to solve a problem, depending on the type of problem and subject matter. Methods that you can try include the following.

- Think about alternative ways to describe the problem.

- View the problem from various perspectives.

- Compare different accounts or explanations of the same problem.

- Break the problem down into manageable parts and omit irrelevant information.

- Try to supply alternatives or different outcomes.

- Try role play or role reversal if appropriate to the problem.

- Recognize important questions to ask about the problem.

- Ask 'What if...?'

- Consider the consequences.

Tip If you are struggling to solve a problem, try to explain it to someone else. This will help you to understand the problem and the other person may be able to offer further insight.

Hypothesizing and theorizing

Students on most courses will need to ask questions and solve problems. If you are on a more advanced course you will need to take this further by understanding how to hypothesize and theorize.

In the traditional science view, a hypothesis is an idea about a phenomenon or observation that is put forward for testing. At this stage it is tentative and not proven. However, once it has been tested repeatedly and the probability of error has been greatly reduced, the hypothesis can be developed into a theory (a set of statements or principles devised to explain a group of facts or phenomena).

Deductive theory generation

The type of theory generation described above is deductive; that is, the theory is deduced from the hypothesis that is developed and tested by the scientist. For a theory to stand up to scientific scrutiny, evidence for its development must be shown clearly and it must be able to explain existing phenomenon and make predictions about the future.

In this view there are four main stages that you would need to work through to develop your theory.

1. Ask questions in the form of a hypothesis.
2. Look for patterns to support or disprove your hypothesis.
3. Formulate your theory, based on the hypothesis.
4. Design experiments to test your theory.

Inductive theory generation

There is another type of theory generation that uses inductive methods. Procedures for inductive theory generation can vary depending on the methodological standpoint of the researcher (see Chapter 17). As a general guide you would need to work through the following stages:

1. Begin your enquiry by observing a phenomenon or behaviour.
2. Develop your research questions based on these observations.
3. Answer these questions through more in-depth observation or questioning.
4. Develop your theory, based on these in-depth observations.
5. Test and modify your theory with further observation.

Reasoning deductively and inductively

As we have seen, it is possible to generate theory deductively and inductively. Both these procedures involve the ability to 'reason'; that is, the ability to think analytically about an issue and arrive at a conclusion or opinion. Deductive reasoning is a process of arriving at a conclusion based on previously known facts, whereas inductive reasoning involves a process of arriving at a conclusion based on observation.

It is important to note that both types of reasoning can go wrong. Therefore, an awareness of the problems that can occur will help you to think more about the development of your own thoughts, hypotheses and theories, and will help you to think more about what you are reading and critiquing (see below). The following examples will help you to understand this more clearly.

Example 1: Deductive reasoning

A commuter arrives at the train station at 8.35, but concludes that he has missed his train because it leaves at 8.30 every morning. He returns home.

Critique

The premise on which the commuter's actions are based is wrong. Although his train may leave at 8.30 every morning and he believes this to be a known fact, this does not mean that it will most certainly leave at this time on the day that he is late. The train could be delayed, the timetable could have changed or there may be another train available.

Deductive reasoning can only be sound if the premise on which it is based is true. When evaluating work, you need to know the premise on which deductive reasoning is based, check that it is true, and work through the reasoning to make sure that the conclusion is valid.

Example 2: Inductive reasoning

A parent notices that their child 'goes a bit weird' when it is a full moon. They speak to other parents who say that their children 'go a bit funny' when it is a full moon. Their conclusion is that children are adversely affected by the full moon.

Critique

The conclusion is a generalization. What children are affected? Does this mean all children in the town, country or in the world? What does 'adversely' mean? What methods were used when speaking to other parents? How many parents were spoken to? What questions were used? Did the parent introduce bias, perhaps by pointing out, first, that their child 'goes a bit weird' during a full moon (see below)? What is meant by 'weird' and 'funny'? How do different parents define these words? Was the parent right to draw this conclusion?

Recognizing bias

'Bias' is a term that is used to describe a tendency or a preference for a particular line of thought, idea, perspective or result. 'Research(er) bias' is used to describe a problem with how the research has been chosen, conducted and/or analysed. For example, in Example 2 above, researcher bias could have been introduced into the process when a parent suggested to other parents that their child 'goes a bit weird' during a full moon.

As a student you need to be able to recognize bias in your work and the work, thoughts, ideas and research of others. To do this it is important to have an awareness of objectivity and subjectivity. This will help you to analyse ideas and concepts, recognize bias and enable you to make judgements about what you are reading. It will also help you to conduct your own research (see Chapter 17).

Objectivity

In scientific terms, objectivity is taken to mean knowledge or theory that is free from bias. To achieve this it must have passed rigorous tests for validity and reliability. There are many tests that purport to do this and scientists must follow strict rules if they are to have their work taken seriously by the scientific community. (Validity refers to the strength of conclusions, inferences or propositions, whereas reliability refers to the consistency of measurement.)

Subjectivity

Subjectivity is often described as being 'of a person'. Everything that makes us who we are influences our knowledge and theory generation. This may include our background, our likes and dislikes, the society and culture in which we live and the historical context in which we are working and studying.

Don't fall into the trap of thinking that subjective work produces 'bad' science. Some very important subjective work has been produced, with all external and internal influences acknowledged. Indeed, some researchers believe that, as we are all human, it is impossible not to introduce subjectivity into our work.

Tip Recognizing bias involves a careful process of thought and analysis. You need to look at the evidence and think about how the evidence was gathered and how it is presented. This is the case for both objective and subjective work. Both can involve bias and through careful analysis you should be able to spot when this occurs.

Critiquing and reviewing

Understanding how to recognize bias will help you to critique the work of other people. Critiquing and reviewing can be a major component of undergraduate courses, especially in the arts and social sciences.

When critiquing and reviewing the work of others, you will find the task easier if you break it down into a series of steps.

- Step 1: Read through the text quickly to get a general idea of the content.

- Step 2: Check the meaning of any unfamiliar words or phrases, using the glossary or your dictionary.

- Step 3: Jot down a few notes about what you think the author is trying to say.

- Step 4: List any questions that have formed in your mind as a result of this preliminary reading.

- Step 5: Return to the text and read it more slowly, asking what the author is trying to prove. A good author will hint at this in the introduction and summarize in the conclusion.

- Step 6: When you have discovered the main point (or points) the author is making, jot it down.

- Step 7: Think about this point (or thesis). Has the author backed up the point with evidence? Is this evidence adequate? Is it convincing? Are you convinced by what you are reading?

- Step 8: Think about the purpose of the text. Why has the author published the work? Who is the paper aimed at?

- Step 9: Think about the research methods. What methods did the author use to develop this thesis? Are the methods sound and appropriate to the topic? Can you think of any problems or an alternative method that might produce different results?

Tip Although, at first, you may find it daunting to review and critique the work of others, you will find that this becomes easier as your course progresses and your subject knowledge, confidence and academic abilities improve.

Summary

Thinking skills are crucial to the success of your studies. Your ability to think well will develop as your course progresses, but you can aid this process by understanding how you think and by making sure that you choose the most appropriate methods for the subject/task. When developing your thinking skills it is important to understand how to recognize objectivity, subjectivity and bias. This will help you to reason, hypothesize and theorize. It will also enable you to critique and review the work of others.

Much of the thinking that you carry out during your studies will be undertaken on an individual basis, during independent study. As a student, being able to study independently is an important skill to develop, and this is discussed in the next chapter.

9 Studying independently

When you move from school to college, and perhaps on to university, you will be required to undertake some independent study. This means that you are responsible for organizing, planning and undertaking your own studies.

To do this successfully you need to know how to plan your work, understand how and where to find information and be able to organize, manage and store the information that you find. You also need to remain motivated. This chapter provides information about these issues.

Planning your independent study

Chapter 2 provides information about managing your time, juggling work, study and play, completing coursework, meeting deadlines and preparing a study plan. If you take note of this advice you will be able to better plan your independent study. When you do this, you should also take note of the following points.

▪ You are responsible for your own learning: no one else can help plan your work for you. It is possible to seek advice when required, but ultimately success or failure is down to you.

▪ Although independent study means that you are responsible for managing your time and organizing your studies, it does not mean that you spend the whole time studying alone. Instead, it means that you are able to work on your own when you need to, but also know when to seek advice from others when required. This could include seeking help from your tutor, IT technicians, librarians and fellow students.

▪ If you are finding it hard to make the transition from teacher-centred learning (common in schools) to student-centred learning, speak to your tutor. He or she will be able to offer advice about planning and undertaking independent study.

Knowing where to start

Tutors understand that it can be difficult for some students to make the transition to independent learning. Therefore, they provide as much help and advice as possible to new students. You should take advantage of the help offered, as this will make your transition easier.

Most colleges and universities have an introduction/orientation week that aims to orient new students geographically, academically and socially. During this time you will be able to take part in guided tours of the learning facilities, and find out more about the social and leisure facilities. You will also have the chance to meet key staff and fellow students. Try to take part in as many activities as possible, as these are all designed for your benefit (see quotation below).

> 'It was great, loads of stuff like library tours...yes, they showed us
> the computers and how to find the books...'cos it was massive, much
> bigger than school. Like, yeah, you know, but it was all on the com-
> puter, you know, in the catalogue. If I'd not been shown that it would
> have been hard, you know, to find out how to do it...yes, well, there

was also some social stuff, you know, meeting other students, not just those on my course…so yeah, make sure you do it.'

Greg, Portsmouth University

IT services

At some colleges and universities you will receive information about e-mail accounts and user accounts when you enrol. At others you will need to visit IT services to set yourself up with an account.

You can obtain a wide variety of useful information from the IT helpdesk and website, including information about safe computer use, searching for material online and important IT rules and regulations. Again, the onus is on you to obtain this information for yourself. More information about accessing IT equipment and facilities is provided in Chapter 12.

Conducting library research

The best way to start your library research is to attend the library/learning centre orientation tour at the beginning of your course so that you can find out about all the resources that are available. Also, use the helpdesk or ask a librarian for help if you are struggling to find a resource or use equipment.

Tip Your reading list is a good place to start as books have been carefully selected by your tutor. Use your list wisely and make sure that you read all texts that are marked as essential reading.

Using library catalogues

All colleges and universities have a computerized library catalogue that enables you to search the entire library stock using a variety of search techniques. It will show you where the book is located and let you know whether it is out on loan. You can use the library catalogue to check your own record of loans, self-renew your books and request other books.

Systems may differ slightly, but in general you should be able to do the following.

- **Log on to the system**. You will need a library card number and password to do this. These are provided during enrolment or are available from the library helpdesk.
- **Perform a quick search**. This enables you to type your search terms and choose the field from a drop-down menu. You can search by keyword, title, author, subject, journal title and ISBN.
- **Perform a full search**. This enables you to carry out a more specific search, combining a number of search terms.
- **Consult the display screen**. Your search results will appear on screen and you can work through the list, checking or clicking on those that interest you. Some systems will enable you to store your search results for the duration of your session and others will enable you to send yourself an e-mail if you wish to keep your search results.
- **Review your search history**. Some systems will enable you to do this when you next log on to the system.
- **Put in a hold request**. If you are interested in an item that is on loan, you can request a copy. If the book is popular you will be held in a queue. You can check your progress in the queue through the catalogue system.
- **Renew your library books**. Most libraries will enable you to renew your books through the catalogue system, usually up to four times if they have not been requested by other borrowers.

Staff at the University of Sheffield realize that their student population is much more diverse than it once used to be. In order to cater for students who have other commitments, such as family or employment, they have decided to open their library 24 hours a day, 7 days a week, for 365 days a year. In 2009 it was reported that at least 40 students visited the library on Christmas Day.

Accessing resources in other libraries

In addition to using your own college or university library, you might wish to consider other options for more in-depth research. The British Library is the national library of the United Kingdom. The collection includes 150 million items with a further 3 million items incorporated every year. For more information consult their website: www.bl.uk.

Copac is a service that gives free access to the online catalogues of universities in the United Kingdom. Consult the website to access the service and to obtain more information: www.copac.ac.uk.

Your library may offer an inter-lending and document supply service that enables you to access books, journals, maps and documents from other university libraries if they are not available in your library. Most libraries will place a limit on the amount of requests that you are able to make and you may be charged for the service. Contact your library helpdesk for more information.

Conducting online research

College and university websites give information about how to use the web carefully and sensibly for your research and you should read their guidelines before you begin your independent study.

When you're surfing the net, there are some extra precautions that you can take to check the reliability and quality of the information you have found.

- Try to use websites run by organizations that you know and trust.

- Check the 'About Us' section for more information about the creator and organization.

- Ask why the website has been set up. What is its purpose? Who is the author? What is their reason for making sure that their information is in the public domain? Can you believe everything presented? What evidence is available to back up claims made on the site?

- Use another source, if possible, to check information. For example, journal articles and books can provide a useful resource when you want to check the reliability of online sources. This is because many journal articles and some books have to be peer-reviewed before they are published. Editors and publishers try to make sure that information is reliable before publishing. This is a more rigorous process than providing information on the internet, which can be done by anyone without any checks.

- You should check the national source of data as information may differ between countries.

Organizing, managing and storing information

Being able to organize and manage information is an essential part of independent study. You will spend much of your time searching for and collecting information for essays, assign-ments, seminar papers, research projects and dissertations. Once you have collected this information, you must be able to organize and manage it so that you are able to retrieve infor-mation when required, and can use what you have found to revise for tests and examinations.

Chapter 6 provides advice on organizing paper and elec-tronic notes. If you are interested in using software to help you to organize, manage and store your information, see Appendix 3. You can also visit your IT services department or consult their website for more information about the software that is available for your use.

Tip Keep proper back-ups of all your work on CD or external memory device as well as your hard disk. This includes all your background research, sources of information and any written work.

Remaining motivated

Remaining motivated is essential to successful independent study. The following advice should help you to keep motivated.

- Choose a course and/or modules in which you have a high level of interest. Don't choose a course just because your parents think it is important or because you think it will help you to get a good job. If you are interested in what you are studying, you will find it easier to remain motivated and you will find your studies more fulfilling and enjoyable.

- Choose assignment/project topics that interest you, as again, this will help you to remain motivated. If you are not interested in a topic you will find it harder to undertake the required work.

- ▨ Ask friends and family not to distract you when you are working. Often it is useful to find a quiet study place away from friends and family, such as a quiet corner of the library/learning centre.

- ▨ Divide your independent study time into manageable chunks and avoid long study sessions that make you tired. Intersperse tedious tasks with more enjoyable tasks.

More information about increasing personal motivation is provided in Chapter 22.

Summary

Studying independently is all about taking control of your time and your studies, understanding where and how to find information and remaining motivated. Tutors realize that some students find it difficult to make the transition from teacher-centred learning to student-centred learning, so they provide as much help and support as possible for new students. You should take advantage of this support as it will help you to develop your independent study skills and use services and facilities more effectively.

There are a variety of independent study skills that you will need to develop, depending on your chosen subject. For example, if you are interested in the sciences you will need to know how to get the most from scientific materials and software, conduct experiments and improve your observation skills. These issues are discussed in the next chapter.

10 Improving your scientific skills

If you want to improve your scientific skills you will need to know how to read scientific material and understand how to analyse and critique what you are reading. You will also need to understand how to interpret charts, tables and graphs, know about the scientific method, conduct experiments, improve your observation skills and know how to write scientific reports. These issues are discussed in this chapter.

Reading scientific material

Although many scientific texts contain a large amount of facts and figures, you shouldn't feel compelled to wade through the text in a logical, sequential order. Instead, you will find it more useful to skim and scan the material, spending extra time on the relevant sections and moving quickly through the less relevant information. This will enable you to cover a greater number of texts and your comprehension of what is being discussed will improve.

The following points will help you to skim and scan scientific material more effectively.

■ Skim through the material to get an overview of the ideas presented. Pay particular attention to the introduction, summary and conclusion.

▪ Try to build up an overview of the information first by scanning the relevant sections and working out how they all fit together. Look for key words or phrases that aid comprehension and help you to piece together what you are reading.

▪ When you skim and scan a text, be aware of words or terms that are new to you. Try to find a definition within the text, but if not, refer to a glossary or dictionary. Keep a record of the term and definition, including the page number within the text, as this will help you when you revise for examinations.

▪ Try to understand what you are reading rather than memorize facts. You will need to memorize some information, but you will find this easier to do if you understand what you are trying to remember.

▪ Cover up some of the material you are reading and work through the ideas or figures in your head. This will aid understanding.

Tip Pay particular attention to charts and figures as these tend to summarize the major ideas and facts that are being presented.

Questioning scientific information

As with all academic work, when you are presented with scientific information you need to approach it from a critical perspective. Therefore, when you read a scientific text, ask the following questions.

1. Who is the author and what are their credentials? What reason have they got for making sure that their information is available?

2. Have they followed the correct procedures when forming hypotheses, experimenting and reaching conclusions? Are their methods well documented and can their experiments be repeated (see 'scientific method' on the next page)?

3. Have the conclusions been scrutinized, tested and verified by other scientists? If not, would it be possible for others to do so?

4. Are the measurements consistent (through repetition and retest)?

5. Have assumptions/conclusions been made that are not based on careful experimentation and analysis?

6. Have generalizations been made that are not based on careful experimentation and analysis?

7. Has bias been introduced in any of the information? This could be during the hypothesis-forming stage, the experimentation stage, the data collection and analysis stage or when making conclusions and writing up results (see Chapter 8).

'When students arrive they seem quite surprised that they should question all the information they are given, especially in science subjects where they tend to believe that everything they are told is true. I give them a text and ask them to dissect it and be as critical as they possibly can be. Some find this very difficult but I show them that some of the best science is based on critiques of other scientists' work.'

Anna, Bournemouth and Poole College

Understanding charts, tables and graphs

Although some scientific charts, tables and graphs may appear complex and confusing, you should not feel over-whelmed. Instead, consider the following points as these will help you to work through the information.

▪ Look first at the main headings. Do they give you an idea of what the table, chart or graph is about?

▪ Look at the headings in each column or the titles on the axes. Are you clear about what is included in each of these columns?

▪ Scan the table or graph for interesting figures or anomalies.

▪ Can you see any particular trends? What do they mean?

▪ What are the high and low points? Why might this be?

▪ Are there any blips or unusual figures? What do they show? Why might this have occurred?

▪ Pick a figure inserted into one part of the table or on the graph. Try to work out what the figure is telling you.

▪ Summarize the main conclusions.

Tip If you are struggling to understand a diagram or figure, write down any ideas you have as it helps you to move your thinking from abstract numbers to written material, which can aid understanding.

Knowing about the scientific method

The scientific method is a method of investigation based on prediction, experiment and observation. It is used to discover new knowledge or to correct, or add to, existing knowledge. Using this method, various steps are followed to discover knowledge.

1. Identify the problem that needs solving.

2. Formulate a hypothesis (a proposed explanation for an observable phenomenon).

3. Test the hypothesis (through experimentation).

4. Collect and analyse the data (through observation and careful recording).

5. Repeat any of the previous steps, if required.

6. Make conclusions.

The steps taken must be repeatable and well documented so that they can be tested and scrutinized by other scientists. This enables others to reproduce the tests and verify the results.

Conducting experiments

If you have to conduct experiments, the procedures vary as they depend on the subject and level of your course, the requirements of your tutor and the equipment available to you. However, as a general guide, you may be required to do the following.

- Think about a title for your work. Your title should describe the nature of your experiment in a clear, concise way. It should be meaningful and easily understood.

- Write a statement of your purpose. This should be short and succinct, describing clearly what you intend to do in your experiment. This will help you to focus your thoughts.

- Think about your methods. How do you intend to conduct your experiment? What are the different stages?

- Gather information about your topic. This may require a literature search, a review of lecture notes or discussion with tutors and other students.

- Identify and summarize significant points from the literature or from your discussions.

▓ Form a hypothesis. This is a statement about a phenomenon or observation that is put forward for testing (see Chapter 8).

▓ Decide what experiments are needed to test your hypothesis.

▓ Design your experiments. When you do this you may need to consider the following points:

– What materials do you require?

– Where will you obtain the materials?

– What are the health and safety considerations for you and others around you?

▓ Conduct your experiments. This may involve the following, depending on the type of experiment:

– Changing one variable in each experiment.

– Accurate recording and measurement of results.

– Repetition of tests to verify findings.

▓ Summarize results.

▓ Draw conclusions.

▓ Write up your results.

Obtaining results

When you are conducting experiments you need to be aware that not all of them will be successful or produce the hoped-for results (see Table 3). This does not mean that you have failed as it is still possible to learn from unsuccessful experiments. They help you to modify and build on your hypothesis until you are able to produce more successful results.

Table 3. Avoiding mistakes in experiments.

Mistake	Action
Presuming that the hypothesis is right, without testing thoroughly	Although a hypothesis may appear right, because it is obvious or common sense, it should still be tested thoroughly. Unexpected results can often occur
Designing a poor experiment because there is a mismatch between tests and purpose	Make sure that the test you intend to conduct fits your statement of purpose. If in doubt, seek advice from your tutor
Introducing researcher bias, due to a desire to succeed, lack of confidence or stubbornness	Make sure that your emotions don't influence your experiments. Understand what is meant by researcher bias (see Chapter 8)
Introducing research bias, due to incorrect procedures or lack of understanding	Make sure that you understand and follow all procedures. Ask your tutor for help if in doubt. Understand what is meant by research bias (see Chapter 8)
Failing to spot important errors	Improve your observation skills (see next page). Be vigilant and keep accurate records of all experiments
Ignoring data that doesn't support your hypothesis	Remain observant and report all results, whether or not they support your hypothesis. Reformulate your hypothesis, if necessary
Falsifying tests and/or results due to a desire to succeed, laziness or incompetence	Keep up to date with your work. Read around the subject. Seek advice if you are struggling. Don't be tempted to falsify results as this will be spotted easily by your tutor/examiner

Improving your skills of observation

Good observation skills are extremely important to scientists, especially when conducting experiments. You can improve your observation skills by taking note of the following.

- Observation skills will improve with patience and practice.

- Observation skills will become more focused if you have some knowledge of what you are observing. Therefore, you need to prepare well for experiments and research tasks that require you to observe. Read around the subject and discuss the issues with your tutor and fellow students.

- Keep comprehensive notes about everything you observe. It is very easy to forget what you have seen when you have other things on your mind. Also, if you don't keep comprehensive notes, observer bias can creep in when you try to remember what has happened at a later date.

- Observe with an open mind. Try not to expect to see something. Instead, wait for something to happen, observing all the time.

Writing scientific reports and papers

When you write a scientific paper or report, you need to keep the aim in mind (to communicate information). You also need to think about your audience and make sure that it is written at the correct level and pitch. Your tutor will offer advice about getting this right for the particular level of your course.

Writing style and structure

Scientific reports and papers usually contain the following sections:

- title;
- abstract;
- introduction;
- methods;
- results;
- discussion;
- conclusion;
- references;
- appendices.

More details about the information that should be included in each of these sections are provided in Chapter 18.

Your writing should follow a logical order, with one paragraph flowing into the next. Pay close attention to grammar, spelling and vocabulary, ensuring that you understand all terminology used. Make sure that your work is consistent and tidy.

When including figures, graphs, tables and charts, make sure that they are all numbered and titled and ensure that all columns and axes are correctly labelled. Figures should be placed within your text, after the paragraph in which they have been mentioned, or they can all be included together in an appendix at the end of your report.

Using science software and online tools

Today there is a wide variety of science software and online tools to help you in your studies. This includes software that enables you to read, view, visualize or break down information, ideas and concepts into a more simple form.

Using this type of software you can obtain a simplified abstract view of complex reality (a model) and bring a model to life, showing how a particular object or phenomenon will behave (a simulation). You can also use visualization software and tools to create images, diagrams or animations to communicate a message.

Speak to your tutor or visit your college/university IT services to find out what science software is available for your use. You can also enter 'free science software' into your search engine to be directed to the wide variety of freely available software and online tools.

Tip Note that a theory is universal, whereas a model is valid only within defined limits.

Summary

As a student on a science course it is important that you know how to read and critique scientific material and understand about the scientific method. This will help you to conduct your own successful experiments and analyse and critique the work of others. You will also need to improve your observation skills and know how to make conclusions and write up your results in the correct way, without introducing bias into the process.

Students on most sciences courses, and a variety of other courses, may also need to develop their mathematical skills. Information on how to do this is provided in the following chapter.

11 Improving your mathematical skills

Most students will need to have a basic understanding of mathematics, even if they are not studying on a mathematics course. This includes an understanding of averages, percentages, fractions and statistics. You may also be required to use mathematical diagrams, cope with problem sheets, take mathematics tests and use mathematical software. These issues are discussed in this chapter.

Calculating averages and percentages

If you have to deal with numerical data on your course, you will need to have a basic understanding of averages and percentages. This is of particular importance for students who have to conduct social research as part of their studies (see Chapter 17).

Averages

In mathematics, if you want to find a simple average of your data you add up the values and divide by the number of items. This is called an arithmetic mean. This is a straightforward calculation used where specific figures can be added together and then divided.

However, it is possible to mislead with averages, especially when the range of the values may be great or there are extreme examples. Mathematicians, therefore, also describe the mode, which is the most frequently occurring value in the data, and the median, which is the middle value of the range. The mode is calculated by finding the number that occurs most often and the median is calculated by putting the values into order and then finding the middle value.

Using means, modes and medians

The mean is used in interval scales when the data is not skewed by extreme values. Interval scales come in the form of numbers with precisely defined intervals and precise comparisons can be made. Examples include answers from questions about age, height and number of children.

The mode is used when dealing with nominal scales. In this type of scale the categories include everyone in the sample; no one should fit into more than one category and the implication is that no one category is better than another. Examples of this type of scale include religious preference, race and gender.

The median is used in interval scales (when data is skewed) and in ordinal scales. For ordinal scales answers can be placed on a continuum, with the implication being that some categories are better than others. In this type of scale it is not possible to measure the difference between the specific categories. An example of this type of scale is the occupationally-based social scale that runs from professional to unskilled manual.

Example

Data in interval scales may be skewed where there are extreme examples, such as salary levels where one person's income is ten times that of another. In this case, the median would be a more appropriate calculation than the mean.

Percentages

Conducting the types of calculations described above can be problematic for mathematicians and researchers when there is missing data (for example, some people may not want to answer a question about age or household income). It is possible to overcome the problem of missing data by converting frequency counts to percentages, which are calculated after excluding missing data. However, percentages can be misleading if the total number of respondents is fewer than 40.

If you want to know more about percentages and how they are calculated and used, you may find it useful to work your way through the 'Ratio, proportion and percentages' unit, available free of charge from the Open University free resources website (http://openlearn.open.ac.uk). Alternatively, speak to your tutor to find out what courses are available at your college/ university.

Tip There are a number of percentage calculators available online (e.g. www.percentagecalculator.net) but it is also useful to have a basic understanding of the calculation techniques involved, especially when analysing your own research data.

Using fractions

Recently, a surprising number of tutors have reported that their students have arrived at university without a basic understanding of fractions. Some believe that this is because students have been taught to use a calculator to perform actual calculations, rather than understand how fractions work before calculations are made.

If you struggle with fractions you may find it useful to work your way through the 'Numbers, units and arithmetic' unit, available free of charge from the Open University free resources website (http://openlearn.open.ac.uk). This unit will help you to revise whole numbers, decimals and fractions, both positive and negative. It will also help you to know when and how to add, subtract, multiply and divide. The course should take five hours to complete and is aimed at introductory level. Alternatively, speak to your tutor to find out what help is available at your college/university.

Making use of statistics

A basic understanding of statistical techniques is important for students who have to deal with numerical data on their course and/or who wish to undertake a research project that requires quantitative data analysis (see Chapter 17).

There are two main categories of statistics.

1. **Descriptive statistics**. These describe or summarize the data and can be numerical or non-numerical. For example, numerical data could include age, height, annual salary and time taken to travel a distance. This data can be presented in a table, chart, graph or as a numerical calculation, such as working out percentages or finding the average (see page 106).

2. **Inferential statistics**. These statistics are used by researchers to analyse samples and draw conclusions. For example, researchers might find that 52% of their sample intends to vote Conservative and that this has risen by 12% since the last opinion poll.

It is not possible to go into any great depth about statistical techniques in this book. However, if this is an area that interests you, useful further reading is provided at the end of this chapter. More information about qualitative and quantitative research methods is provided in Chapter 17.

Using data analysis software

If you have computing software available you should find that this is the easiest and quickest way to analyse your data (see below). Most colleges and universities run statistics and data analysis courses, and/or IT services will provide information leaflets and training sessions on data analysis software. Speak to your tutor to find out what is available.

Alternatively, you might find it useful to work your way through the 'Getting started with SPSS' unit, available free of charge from the Open University free resources website (http://openlearn.open.ac.uk). This unit takes a step-by-step approach to statistics software through seven interactive activities, and you don't need statistics software to complete the unit.

Using mathematical diagrams

In mathematics, diagrams tend to be used in four ways.

1. Picture diagrams that represent objects in the real world. Pictures don't need to be drawn to scale (although it may help to approximate dimensions) and don't need to include a great amount of detail. Instead, they are just a representation of the object. Drawing this type of picture can help you to visualize a problem and find a solution.

2. Graphs and charts that use two-dimensional images to show relationships between various and varying quantities. More information about graphs and charts is provided in Chapter 10.

3. Process diagrams that show a series of steps, or logical sequence, to illustrate an idea, concept or point. This type of diagram includes flow charts, for example, and can be useful to aid your understanding of processes.

4. Concept diagrams that provide an abstract representation of an idea, concept or point. This type of diagram can help you to understand a complex idea.

Questioning numerical information

When you are presented with numerical information, such as statistics or the types of diagrams described above, you need to ask questions to determine the nature, strength and proof of the information.

▓ Can you put the data into context, for example, by relating it to something you have seen, heard or read before?

▓ Is the data what you might expect?

▓ Can it be reproduced?

▓ What methods have been employed to obtain the data?

▓ Have all cases, possibilities and alternatives been considered?

▓ Have any assumptions/generalizations been made that cannot be backed up by the evidence?

▓ What is the theorem? (This is a statement that has been proved to be true. Validity has been established and proven.)

▓ What is the proof? (This is a formal argument used to demonstrate the validity of a statement or theorem.)

Coping with problem sheets

For some mathematics, statistics and data analysis courses you will be required to complete problem sheets. The following tips should help you to do this.

■ Make sure that you understand thoroughly what you are being asked to do. If you don't understand what is required, ask your tutor for clarification.

■ Begin working on problem sheets as soon as possible and complete them even if they are not assessed, as this will aid understanding.

■ Always work through problem sheets before the seminar/class is held on the topic. The class will make more sense and you will be able to clarify issues and pick up on points that you don't understand.

■ Many problems can be solved through the use of a good diagram or model. This will help you to simplify and interpret the problem (see page 110).

■ Write down what you are doing. This aids comprehension and enables you to retrace your steps, if required.

■ If you are presented with multiple-choice questions, make sure that you read all the options before you decide on your answer (see Chapter 20).

■ Try brainstorming with other students to help you work through difficult questions.

Tip Remember that even if you get a question wrong, you have learned a lot just by trying to solve the problem.

Taking mathematical tests

Chapter 20 provides advice and guidance about taking different types of tests during your studies. In addition to this advice, you should take note of the following when taking maths or statistics tests.

▪ Make sure that you read all the instructions carefully and answer the right number of questions. Always read the whole question carefully and don't make assumptions about what is required.

▪ Complete the easiest questions first as this will help your confidence. If you can't answer a question, skip over it and return later if you have time.

▪ Show all your workings, and write clearly so that everything can be understood by the marker. If you don't want the marker to take some of your workings into account, make sure that they are erased or crossed out clearly.

▪ Don't erase your workings if you can't find the right answer, or you know that your answer is wrong. You may still obtain some marks for your workings.

▪ Once you have completed the test, check your answers carefully. If you have time, work through some of the more difficult questions again, to determine whether you arrive at the same answer.

Using mathematical software and online tools

There is a wide variety of mathematical tools and software available, many of which are free to use. This includes useful calculators, modelling, visualization and simulation software and real-time data collection software. Also, your college or university will provide mathematical and statistical software that will help with data analysis. Speak to your tutor or visit IT services at your institution to find out what is available.

If you are struggling with any aspects of mathematics, there are many online tutorials available to help you to work through your difficulties. As we have seen in this chapter, some of the best are available from the Open University free resources website (http://openlearn.open.ac.uk). See Appendix 3 for more information about other software that is available.

If you prefer to work with other students under guided supervision, speak to your tutor or contact the study support unit at your college or university to find out what help is available. See Appendix 2 for more information about study skills support.

Summary

Most students will need a basic understanding of mathematics, even if they are not studying on a mathematics or scientific course. Although it is possible to find software and online tools that will help you to work out most types of calculation, it is desirable to have a basic understanding of the methods, formulas and rules, especially if you have to conduct your own data analysis. It is also important to understand how to interpret, analyse and critique data. Courses are provided by your college/university and online to help you to learn more.

All colleges and universities have mathematical, statistical and other types of software available that is free for students. To get the most out of this software you need to develop your IT skills. These issues are discussed in the following chapter.

Further reading

Elliot, J. and Marsh, C., *Exploring Data: An introduction to data analysis for social scientists*, 2nd edition (Cambridge: Polity Press, 2008).

12 Using information technology

Colleges and universities provide a wide variety of IT equipment and facilities for students' use and you may also choose to take your own PC/laptop to college or university. The efficiency and effectiveness of your studies can be greatly enhanced through developing your IT skills and through prudent use of IT equipment, software and facilities. These issues are discussed in this chapter.

Making the most of IT equipment and facilities

The IT equipment and services available will vary between institutions. However, most university and college IT services will provide some or all of the equipment and services listed below:

- a campus network of PCs, some with twenty-four-hour access;
- workstations and laboratories;
- advice and helpdesk service;
- printing and binding services;
- e-mail;
- network connection service;

Using the internet at college and university

All students can access the internet at their college or university free of charge. However, some learning providers may limit the amount of time you can spend online and others will limit the amount of space you are given to store the information you have downloaded.

All learning providers will have strict rules about obscene material, software theft, breach of copyright and plagiarism. You should obtain a list of rules and regulations from IT services. More information about e-learning, e-resources and plagiarism can be obtained from www.jisc.ac.uk.

Connecting your PC/laptop

Many college and university study bedrooms and some libraries and study rooms have connection points for linking to the internet and the university network. Also, many institutions now have wireless connection. Guidelines for connecting your computer will be provided by IT staff. Before you can connect to the campus network, universities will insist that your computer is secure, which means that you will need:

- the latest operating system updates;
- up-to-date virus protection;
- a firewall enabled;
- a system password set;
- safe computing configuration (this includes issues such as breach of copyright, securing against identity theft and spyware, and problems with information disclosure on social networks).

- audiovisual equipment;
- remote access services;
- file recovery service;
- assistance and training in ICT use;
- a computer shop selling hardware and software tional prices;
- sanitized equipment for resale to students.

When you choose a learning provider, consult their p tus and website to find out what equipment will be a for your use. Many IT services departments will hav own website that lists the available equipment.

Obtaining IT information and advice

If you attend an open day you should be shown what e ment is available for your use. Always attend library/lear centre tours at the start of your course as these will help y become familiar with the services and equipment. All libra will have a helpdesk or reception available where you seek general or specialist advice.

Once you enrol on your course, visit IT services. They have a helpdesk where you will be able to ask questions a pick up leaflets about the available equipment and service Also, many colleges and universities run additional IT trainin sessions for students. Contact your tutor or IT services fo more information.

Tip Students studying on computing courses are a good source of free IT help, advice and information.

Networking and communicating

Your college/university will have an intranet, which is a set of networks under the control of a single administration. It is usually a local area network (LAN), which connects computers and devices in a limited geographical area, or a campus area network (CAN), which can cover a variety of campus buildings over a larger geographical area.

College and university intranets are used to communicate and pass on all the information you will require while you are studying. This includes information about accommodation, bars, eating places, religion, the library, IT services, childcare, shops, health and safety issues, medical facilities, financial information and study skills. When you enrol you will be given a username and password to access the intranet. This should be your first port of call when you need specific information about your college or university.

Most colleges and universities will also have a virtual learning environment (VLE) and these are discussed in Chapter 13.

Obtaining an e-mail account

Many colleges and universities register new students automatically for their central e-mail system. If this is not the case, contact staff at IT services, who will issue you with an e-mail address for their system. You will be given a login code (or username) and password, which you will need to remember in addition to your e-mail address.

Different e-mail systems are structured in different ways. When you register, ask staff how you get started on the system. Also, your learning provider will have strict rules and regulations about using e-mail. Make sure that you read these before you start using the facilities. In most places sending offensive messages or material that belongs to other people is considered a serious offence.

Contacting your tutor

Your tutors will let you know how they prefer you to communicate with them at the beginning of the course. For some courses you will have a number of personal tutorials during which you can meet your personal tutor face-to-face to discuss your course and any other issues of concern. Other tutors will provide you with their e-mail address and/or a daytime contact number. Others will request that you make contact through the departmental administration team. Remember that most tutors are extremely busy and will not be able to respond instantly to your request (see quotation below).

> 'Obviously students work all hours, often through the night. On occasions I've had a student e-mail me at 3.30 a.m. and expect an immediate response. I only look at my e-mail first thing in the morning (9 a.m., if I'm not lecturing) and last thing at night (5 p.m., if I'm not lecturing). Sometimes I get up to 100 e-mails a day. I'm too busy to respond to them all, so students have to understand that they must be patient. I will get around to them eventually. Students need to plan ahead so that they don't need an urgent response.'
>
> Geoff, Bournemouth University

Receiving communication from your tutor/ department

Tutors choose to make contact with you in a variety of ways, depending on their preferences and the procedures adopted at your college or university. Some will post information on the intranet (see above) whereas others will send e-mail to all their students. Some departments still use noticeboards and pigeonholes to pass on information. Others use blogs and podcasts and these are discussed in Chapter 13.

You should find out the preferred method(s) at your college/university and ensure that you check regularly for tutor/departmental communication so that you don't miss any important information.

Managing and storing folders and documents

As a student you will generate and accumulate a large amount of folders and documents. This includes information you have downloaded, assignments, tables and diagrams, photographs, bibliographies, background notes and tutor feedback. If you are organized from the outset you won't waste valuable time searching for information that is difficult to locate. You can become more organized by taking note of the following.

- Be consistent when naming folders and documents. Use a naming system that is short, clear, concise and easy to understand. Use the same system throughout your course. You can choose to use abbreviations, subjects or download a program that will enable you to 'colour' folders and documents, for easy reference. Store similar work in folders together.

- Make sure that the automatic save facility on your PC or laptop is set to a short timescale. That way, you will not lose much work if anything should happen to your laptop/PC while you are working on an important piece of work. Save your work manually on a regular basis.

- Use shortcuts to access assignments and projects that you are currently working on. Keep current work and older work separate. Tidy your folders on a regular basis, moving older projects and assignments to a different location.

- Back up all your work on a regular basis. It is useful to keep copies at different locations; for example, on your college/university shared network location and a flash drive, external hard drive or on a CD. This will enable you to access your work if the college/university network is down, or if you have problems with your own PC/laptop.

- If you find it helpful, use file management software to help you to organize your files, such as Google Desktop (http://desktop.google.com).

Tip Don't save unnecessary files, such as e-mail or background notes, that you will never use again. This can cause your PC/laptop to run slower over time.

Using databases

Databases are used to organize, store, manage and retrieve information. As a student you might use databases to store research data or addresses/contact details, for example. There are two categories of database: desktop databases (for single users on PCs) and server databases (multi-user applications, available on your college/university network).

If you think a database might be useful to help to store addresses and contact details, you will find a desktop database such as Microsoft Access (http://office.microsoft.com/access) is all you require. However, if you are in your third year of study and are intending to carry out a large survey that will need complex calculations to be performed, you will need to use a server database. Your tutor or IT services will be able to offer advice about what is available for your use, and direct you to relevant information leaflets or training courses.

Using spreadsheets

Spreadsheets enable you to create and manipulate information in tables. As a student, you might find spreadsheets useful for keeping account of your income and expenditure, for example. The most common spreadsheets on the market are Excel (http://office.microsoft.com/excel) and Lotus 1-2-3 (http://www-01.ibm.com/software/lotus/products/123). A new generation of online spreadsheets has also emerged, and some of these are free and open source (see www.software-garden.com and www.extentech.com).

If you are interested in using spreadsheets, your tutor or IT services will be able to offer advice about what is available for your use, and direct you to relevant information leaflets or training courses. There is also a wide variety of free spreadsheets and tutorials available online (see further information on page 125).

Tip   As a student you are entitled to educational discounts on all software and hardware. Visit www.software4students.co.uk and http://students.pugh.co.uk for more information.

Keeping safe

If you have grown up using computers, you should be well aware of safety issues. To reiterate, you should take note of the following.

- Avoid viruses and spyware. Keep you computer current with the latest updates and anti-virus tools; stay informed about recent threats; never open e-mail attachments from someone you don't know or trust; use an internet firewall; use a malware protection program. Make sure that your friends adhere to this advice as viruses are spread among friends via instant messenger and e-mail.

- Use a complicated password that will be difficult to hack and include capital letters and numbers. Change your password regularly. Don't use the same password for different accounts.

- Keep your computer and web browser up to date.

- Back up all important college/university work at regular intervals so that if you do get a virus you won't lose your work.

- Encrypt your wireless network.

For free, expert advice on how to keep safe online, visit www. getsafeonline.org. More information about remaining safe when using online blogs, discussion groups and social networking sites is provided in Chapter 13.

Security on your PC/laptop

If you intend to use your own PC/laptop at college/university, you will find that some learning providers run a clean access service that uses a technology called Network Admission Control. It checks that your computer has valid and up-to-date anti-virus software and that, if you run Windows, it is up to date with security patches.

When you move to college or university your connection will be immediate if your computer is up to date. If not, you will be given a series of information leaflets on how you can make your computer secure and connect to the system. If your chosen college/university runs this type of system you will be given relevant information when you receive your accommodation pack, so you should be able to make sure that your PC/laptop can be connected quickly upon arrival. You may have to sign an acceptable-use policy before you can connect your PC/laptop.

Summary

As a student the effectiveness and efficiency of your studies will be enhanced through developing your IT skills. Colleges and universities provide a large amount of hardware and software that is freely available to students, and there are many free and open-source programmes available to aid your studies. However, it is important to remain safe and avoid problems with viruses and spyware when using IT equipment. All colleges and universities have strict rules and regulations about the use of their facilities, and you should make sure that you become familiar with these when you start your course.

As you become more familiar with the IT equipment and services that are available, you will be able to think more about developing your e-learning skills. These issues are discussed in the following chapter.

Further information

www.openoffice.org

Open Office is an open-source office software suite for word processing, spreadsheets, presentations, graphics, databases, etc. It works on all common computers and can be downloaded and used completely free of charge for any purpose.

13 Using e-learning technologies

'E-learning' is a term that is used to describe learning that arises through the use of new technology in education. It includes, for example, students using a computer to access interactive learning materials in the classroom or from home; the establishment of virtual learning environments by colleges and universities; communication with fellow students and tutors through online discussions and blogs; the use of wikis and podcasts. These issues are discussed in this chapter.

Making the most of e-learning facilities and support

Universities and colleges provide a wide variety of e-learning opportunities for their students. When you enrol on your course you will be given a username and password that will enable you to access the e-learning facilities. Most colleges and universities provide online tutorials that guide you through the available facilities. If not, visit IT services for more information and advice.

> The University of Bradford is developing an 'e-induction' scheme that will enable students to download guides to their mobile phones to help them to prepare for university life. The aim of this new scheme is to enable prospective students to feel at home with campus life before they arrive at university.

The scheme will include a 'self-audit' that will help students to gauge their levels of confidence in different academic areas and with their study skills. From this self-audit, students can develop an action plan that they can work through with their personal tutors. This could include attending training sessions or receiving help from a study support unit.

Keeping up to date with e-learning technologies

There are two important issues regarding keeping up to date with e-learning technologies. The first is that technology is being used more often in the learning environment and to get the most out of this technology (and improve your learning) you need to know how to use it effectively. The second is that if you understand how to keep your personal equipment up to date you will be able to avoid problems with hacking and viruses (see Chapter 12).

All colleges and universities offer advice to students concerning new technology. This may be via their website, from free leaflets and booklets, from training courses, modules and seminars, and through induction sessions. Speak to your tutor to find out what is available at your institution and make sure that you utilize all the available information. This will help you to get the most out of new technology, and help you to develop skills and knowledge that will be useful to you when you look for work after you have completed your studies.

Making the most of virtual learning environments

A virtual learning environment (VLE) is a system designed to facilitate teaching and learning using computers. VLEs are designed to enable learning to take place at any time, any-where, and can be made available for students on campus and for distance learners. In general, VLEs enable you to do the following.

- Access module/subject support information and course handbooks.
- Obtain course evaluation and feedback forms.
- Access learning materials, such as course materials, read-ing lists, case studies and scenarios.
- Submit work online.
- Take part in online discussions with other students and tutors, enabling you to share, build on and exchange knowledge through discussion forums and groups.
- Link to relevant information such as online journals, research reports and useful websites.
- E-mail staff (see Chapter 12).
- Access online training courses and tutorials.
- Read previous examination questions.

Accessing your VLE

To make the most of your VLE you should register as soon as you enrol. Your course information pack or tutor will provide information on how to do this. In most cases you will be able to log on to the system using the same user name and password that you use for your e-mail (see Chapter 12). If you have any problems logging on, contact IT services. Never disclose your password to anyone and change your password on a regular basis.

VLEs contain information files, audio tours and/or short pre-sentations that show you how to use the system. Also, your tutor may have considerable input for their section of the VLE, so speak to your tutor if you are having any difficulty accessing information or submitting work.

On some VLEs you will find that access to certain areas is restricted, usually because the information is available only for staff or students on certain courses.

Improving computing skills

Most young students have grown up using computers and will feel comfortable using the technology. However, if this is not the case, or if you are an adult student who has not had the chance to become familiar with the technology, you need to improve your computer skills to get the most out of e-learning technologies.

Queen Mary, University of London, has recently developed a place called 'The Hive'. This provides an informal learning area with around 50 workstations and wireless access to the Queen Mary Teaching Service. Networked printing facilities are also available. Mobile phone use is tolerated throughout The Hive and students are welcome to bring along their own food and drink. The area has 300 seats across the two spaces, and is aimed at both large and small groups.

Enrolling on a training course

If you wish to enrol on a training course, there are various options available. For example, you may find it useful to enrol on an IT course provided by your college or university. Contact the study support unit, IT services or ask your tutor for guidance.

Alternatively, you may find it useful to enrol on a 'Computers for beginners' or 'Computers for the terrified' course, which are run by your local adult education service. These courses are aimed at people who have no IT experience, and are taught by well-trained tutors who understand that you may be nervous and unconfident. Contact details can be obtained from your local telephone directory.

If you already have some IT knowledge, you may find it useful to work your way through an online tutorial. A good example is the Open University's 'Using a computer for study' course (http://openlearn.open.ac.uk).

Improving online learning skills

If you choose to study an online course, or your tutor requires you to undertake this type of learning as part of your college/university course, you will find that time management is an important skill to learn (see Chapter 2). You will also need to know how to study independently and remain motivated (see Chapter 9). In addition to the advice offered in these two chapters, the following points will help you to study online.

- Make sure that you read, and understand, all instructions. If in doubt, ask for help.

- Define your priorities. When working online it is easy to spend too much time checking or posting to online discussions or sending messages. Decide what needs to be done and stick to your plan.

- Keep copies of all your online work.

- Be mindful of privacy issues. Exercise good judgement when posting or e-mailing confidential information.

Tip For online courses the tutor may not provide reminders regarding online content and assignments, so it is up to you to log on regularly and complete work in your own time.

Learning from podcasts, blogs and wikis

Increasingly, tutors and students are utilizing podcasts, blogs and wikis as a teaching and learning resource. More information about their use will be included in your course materials or can be obtained from your college/university intranet or VLE.

Podcasts

A podcast is a series of digital media files that are released in episodes and downloaded by the target audience. They can be audio or video files and are used in education by tutors to deliver lectures, or provide detailed information on specific themes and subjects. Podcasts help to seed independent learning activity.

In a pilot project, Bournemouth University is encouraging staff to record lectures and upload videos to their website. Managers believe that this will help to solve problems with lectures being cancelled due to staff illness or absence, and that they will be helpful to disabled, international and mature students who have other commitments. So far, more than 200 lectures have been uploaded.

Podcasts of lectures enable you to return to a lecture, listen over again, pick out salient points and take notes on what was missed previously. However, they should not be used as a substitute for attending lectures. Indeed, recent research by the School of Politics and International Studies at the University of Leeds found that the overwhelming majority of students felt that pre-recorded lectures should not be used in place of the traditional lecture.

Blogs

A blog is a website (or page on a website) that is usually maintained by an individual, with entries added on a regular basis. In education, blogs are created by academics and students to discuss specific subjects or pieces of research.

Today there are many leading academics who actively blog and provide trustworthy sources of current opinion and information for students and researchers. Content is controlled by the blog author and they can decide whether or not to receive comments on their blogs. As a student you can read blogs, comment on blogs or write your own blog. Indeed, on some courses you may be asked to blog as part of a marked assignment.

Wikis

Wikis are simple web pages that students, tutors, families and friends can create and edit together. The most well known is Wikipedia (www.wikipedia.org).

When wikis are used in teaching and learning they offer the opportunity for tutors and students to have equal active roles as contributors and editors. They are ideal for collaborative writing projects. However, the content of wikis tends to be open to the public and therefore should not contain sensitive material.

Understanding safety issues

When using online discussions, blogs and wikis, you should take note of the following.

- Use a nickname or your initials instead of your full name and don't post your home address or college/university address.

- Do the 'face-to-face stranger' test. Would you give the information to a stranger you have just met face-to-face in the street? If not, don't include it in your discussion or blog.

- Think about the information you are posting. Would you want it to be read by your parents, a tutor or a future employer? If the answer is no, don't post it.

- Think carefully before uploading pictures as they could be on the net for a very long time and you won't be able to get them back.

- Respect the views of others. Be considerate and don't dominate discussions.

- Don't be tempted to post false information.

- Try to find out whether what you post is correct before submission.

Understanding netiquette

'Netiquette' refers to a set of social conventions that aid and facilitate interaction over networks. For you to get the most out of e-learning facilities and support, it is important that you take note of the following.

- Behave as you would in the classroom. Be punctual, polite and don't dominate discussions.

▪ Try to be yourself. Don't pretend to be something you are not.

▪ Respect the views of others, even if they seem to be less knowledgeable than you or if they break netiquette rules. Challenge ideas rather than challenging people. Let other users know that you have read and appreciate their posts.

▪ DON'T SHOUT (type in capitals). Don't be offensive. Never resort to 'flaming' (personal attacks and insults). Derogatory and personal insults will be dealt with firmly by your college/university, and could result in expulsion.

▪ When sharing ideas, information and knowledge, keep technical jargon to a minimum, explain complex terms, keep to the topic and define acronyms.

▪ Write in complete and logical sentences. Use correct spelling, grammar, capitalization and punctuation.

Tip   Take time to think carefully about, and check over, what you have written before you submit.

Summary

E-learning technologies are moving on at a rapid pace so, to make the most of these facilities while you are studying, you need to keep up to date with developments. E-learning can include the use of VLEs, podcasts, blogs, wikis, discussion groups and online forums. When using this type of technology it is important to understand safety issues and adhere to the rules of netiquette so that you can get the most out of the technology and don't offend others.

Although some of your course content may be delivered with the use of e-learning technologies, in most cases you will still need to attend lectures, seminars, tutorials and/or classes. Getting the most out of these teaching methods is discussed in the following chapter.

14 Getting the most out of lectures, seminars, tutorials and classes

In colleges and universities teaching is delivered through lectures, seminars, tutorials and/or tutor-led classes. A lecture is formal tuition given by a lecturer to a large number of students and often takes place in a lecture theatre. A seminar is a small group discussion on a particular topic (sometimes presented by students). A tutorial is a small group or individual session led by a tutor to discuss a specific topic. In a class, instruction on the topic is provided by the tutor to a small or large group of students.

To get the most out of these sessions you must prepare thoroughly, know how to take and organize notes, learn how to concentrate, review and evaluate your notes and work effectively with your tutor. These issues are discussed in this chapter.

Preparing for lectures, seminars, tutorials and classes

Thorough preparation helps to focus your attention, prepares your mind to receive information and helps you to concentrate fully on the topic. There are four main stages to the preparation process.

1. Review your notes from previous lectures, seminars, tutorials and classes. Read through your notes and try to recall the main points.

2. Read more about the topic. This will aid understanding and help you to retain information because it has more meaning and relevance.

3. Begin to form questions about the topic. Is there anything you don't understand? Is there anything that requires clarification? What do you want to know?

4. Predict what you think will be included in the session, based on your background reading and knowledge of the subject. What do you expect to be covered? What will be the main points?

Tip Through careful preparation you can build on your subject knowledge and understanding. This will enable you to write better assignments and revise more effectively for examinations.

Taking notes effectively

Comprehensive information about taking notes effectively is provided in Chapter 6. In addition to this advice, you should take note of the following.

- If using a laptop to take notes, don't get distracted by checking e-mail, social networking or playing games. You will not only distract yourself, but will also cause disturbance to other students around you.

- Use diagrams to summarize main points, if relevant. Expand on the diagram after the lecture, so that you are clear about what it represents.

▪ Some tutors will provide you with handouts at the start of the session. If this is the case, use the session to expand on the points given in the handout, but make sure that you listen to the tutor, rather than read the handout. You can do this after the session has finished.

▪ If you have missed an important point, ask a question at the end of the session, or try to speak to the tutor. If this is not possible, consult with other students to clarify the issue.

Tip If you are unable to attend a session, speak to the module co-ordinator or your tutor. They will be able to provide you with a list of recommended reading, or direct you to podcasts, lecture notes and/or seminar papers that may be available on the college/university intranet. You can also ask your friends for copies of their notes.

Using technology to record lectures

As we have seen in Chapter 7, there are a variety of digital audio devices that can be used in classes, lectures and seminars. If you choose to use this technology, and you can afford to do so, you should take note of the following points.

▪ If you are working in smaller groups, such as during a seminar or tutorial, you should check that everyone is happy to have the discussion recorded. Some tutors might not allow you to record certain discussions and you should never do so without their consent.

▪ Don't rely solely on the audio device. You must listen to the tutor and take notes as well. This will help you to listen actively, which enables you to understand, evaluate and interpret what you are hearing (see Chapter 7). It also means that if the audio device should fail (due to low batteries or user error, for example) you will still have notes that you can use for assignments and exam revision.

- Practise with the audio device as much as possible, prior to your lectures and seminars. This will help you to minimize potential problems. Become familiar with the device, and understand the limitations, especially in terms of sound range. You may need to sit as close as possible to the tutor for the device to work well.

- Check that the device is fully charged and that the power will last for the duration of the session.

The School of Engineering, Mathematics and Physical Sciences at the University of Exeter has recently built a state-of-the-art 3D lecture theatre. The room is also equipped with software that enables students and tutors to create their own 3D images. The facilities are useful for applications such as climate-change modelling, vegetation mapping and advanced computational fluid dynamics.

Improving concentration

As we have seen in Chapter 7, active listening helps you to maintain concentration. In addition to this, there are other things that you can do to help improve and maintain your concentration during lectures, seminars tutorials and classes.

- Try to maintain the right frame of mind for study. Don't become distracted by personal problems or thoughts about what you intend to do at the weekend.

- Be aware of when your mind wanders to something other than the lecture. Pull your mind back to the subject.

- Don't just listen to what is being said, but try to understand it. Form your own opinions or develop questions to aid your understanding as this will lead to deeper concentration.

- Avoid distractions by sitting in a place that has the least disturbances. In a lecture theatre this tends to be towards the front, in the middle.

- It is much harder to concentrate when you feel tired, run down or ill. Try to remain fit and healthy and make sure that you get plenty of sleep (see Chapter 22).

Knowing when and how to question

Some lecturers don't want students to ask questions during a lecture (see quotation, below). If this is the case, they should make it clear at the start of the lecture/course. However, some will answer questions during a lecture, whereas others will request that all questions are kept until the end, time permitting.

If you have any questions, jot them down so that you can remember what you want to ask when you are able to. If you don't get a chance, but feel the question is really important, keep a note for future reference. You may be able to research the answer yourself (see Chapter 9), or may be able to ask the question in a subject-related seminar or tutorial. Seminars and tutorials are designed to generate discussion, so you should have the opportunity to ask as many questions as you wish.

'We were doing an MA in social research and for one part of the course we had to attend an undergraduate lecture. We were used to asking questions whenever we wanted, so when the lecturer said something we disagreed with, my friend asked for clarification. Well, you could hear the gasp from the other students. The lecturer

just looked at us and said "no questions" and just carried on. We were really surprised at his rudeness, but apparently he told people at the beginning of the course there would be no questions. But we weren't there at the beginning so we didn't know.'

Marion, 42, University of Kent

Reviewing and evaluating

To get the most out of lectures, seminars, tutorials and classes, you need to review and evaluate. Once the session has finished, ask the following questions.

- What were the main points and/or arguments?
- What have I learned so far?
- How does this relate to other sessions?
- How does this relate to information I already know?
- Are there any points about which I am unclear? If so, what am I going to do to clarify the point(s)?

Editing and organizing notes

Once you have reviewed and evaluated, you need to edit and organize your notes. Information and advice about organizing your paper and electronic notes are provided in Chapter 6. In addition to this advice, you should take note of the following.

- Edit and/or expand on your notes as soon as possible after the session, when the information is still fresh in your mind. This is of particular importance if you have used diagrams, charts or pictures to represent the main points. Although you may understand these at the time you have produced them, their meaning may be unclear when you come to revise for exams.

- Expand on any shorthand or abbreviations that you have used. Again, these may be clear to you at the time you attend the session, but may be confusing when you return to your notes several months later.

- As you read through your notes, highlight any important information within the text. This will make it easier to skim and scan for revision. Also, you may find it useful to repeat any important facts and figures in a summary at the end of your notes.

- When you file your notes make sure that you have included the title of the lecture/seminar, the course code, the course name, the lecturer's name and the date. This will ensure that your notes are filed in the correct order and relevant subject file, and will help you to check up any information with the relevant tutor, if required.

Working with your tutor

Tutors want to help their students as much as possible (see quotation below). Therefore, take note of all the information and advice offered by your tutor. Most will provide study skills information, advice about how to take examinations and hint at what will be included in examination questions. Therefore, make sure that you attend all lectures, seminars, tutorials and classes to ensure that you don't miss any important information and advice.

'I teach first- and second-year students. In the first few weeks of the course I offer as much advice as I can about how to complete assignments. I do this before they start to write them and I also offer plenty of feedback once I have marked their work. But students need to realize it is a two-way process. They have to put in the work and they have to act on my advice. If they put in the work I will help them

as much as I can. The best students are those who listen, take notice of what I say and come to me for help if they need it.'

Andrew, Weymouth College

Summary

To get the most out of lectures, seminars, tutorials and classes you need to prepare thoroughly in advance. Read around the topic: your tutor will provide information about guided reading and you can use your independent study skills to read more. You should listen actively and take notes, which you should review, evaluate, edit and organize after the session. Tutors will offer advice, guidance and feedback where appropriate, and your studies will be more successful if you heed their advice.

In addition to attending lectures, seminars, tutorials and classes, you may also need to undertake groupwork. To do this successfully you will need good communication skills and an understanding of group dynamics. These issues are discussed in the following chapter.

Further information

www.videojug.com

Visit the 'family and education' section of this site for videos from lecturers and tutors about attending lectures, seminars and tutorials. Advice is offered about why you should attend, how to get the most out of lectures, how to prepare and how to organize your notes. There are also videos on taking exams, writing essays and improving concentration.

15 Working in groups

Most students studying at colleges and universities will be required to undertake some type of groupwork during their studies. This could include, for example, group project work, where the group has to produce a piece of work that is handed in for assessment, or a group presentation that may or may not count towards course marks. Good communication skills and an understanding of group dynamics are crucial to successful groupwork. These issues are discussed in this chapter.

Improving your group communication skills

Communication is the key to effective groupwork. This involves putting across your message effectively and listening to the messages from other people.

Verbal skills

When you are working in a group you need to be able to convey your thoughts and opinions effectively. You can do this by considering the following points.

- Explain your opinions clearly and concisely. Don't be afraid of pauses if they help you to structure your argument.

▓ Speak slowly as it is easier for you to convey your thoughts and makes it easier for other people to listen to what you have to say.

▓ Don't take things personally when people don't agree with your opinions.

▓ Be patient. If someone doesn't seem to understand what you are saying, try to explain yourself in a different way.

▓ Don't assume that you are right all the time. Be open to other ideas and opinions. However, if you are certain of your views, don't be persuaded by alternative arguments, especially when they are expressed more forcefully than yours.

▓ Be confident and assertive, but not rude or aggressive.

Some people are extremely nervous about talking in front of other people. If this is the case, consult Chapter 21 for advice on conquering nerves when speaking in public.

Listening skills

Being able to listen in a group setting is extremely important, yet it is a skill that some people find very hard. However, we can all recognize when someone is not listening to us or not taking our views seriously.

More information about becoming an effective listener is provided in Chapter 6. In addition to this, when working in a group you need to listen carefully and demonstrate that you are listening to others, through eye contact, nods, agreement and summaries. You should wait for someone to complete their sentence before giving your own thoughts. This will lead to effective and constructive groupwork.

Tip If people know that others are listening to them, they are more likely to continue to offer their thoughts and will be more willing to listen to others.

Planning your groupwork

When planning your groupwork you need to work through some initial questions. These depend on the type and purpose of your group, but could include the following.

* Do you need to appoint a chairperson? If so, how will this person be appointed?

* Do you need to keep a record of events and, if so, who will agree to do this?

* When, where and how regularly is your group going to meet?

* Is it possible and desirable to obtain contact details for each group member?

* Do you need somebody to keep track of time?

* How will you make sure that everybody in the group is able to make a contribution and that their opinions are not ridiculed or undervalued?

* Do people in your group have different strengths and weaknesses? How will you determine this and will it have an influence on the allocation of work (see page 148)?

* What work do you have to complete? Is there a specific deadline?

* How will your conclusions be presented and by whom?

Developing a code of conduct

When a group first meets you have very little idea of how people will interact. Therefore, you can solve problems by setting ground rules (a 'code of conduct') from the start. This should cover:

- the importance of actively listening to each other;

- respecting individual values and opinions;

- discouraging the use of offensive or upsetting language or opinions;

- the allocation of work and the commitment expected from each group member;

- what the group will do if someone doesn't turn up for meetings or doesn't complete their allocated work;

- how you will resolve conflict if it arises;

- issues of confidentiality.

Make sure that every group member is happy with the code and agrees to abide by its rules, then write it on a flip chart or produce a handout. If anyone strays from the rules, a gentle reminder from several group members may be enough to sort out the problem.

Listing aims and objectives

Some groups find it useful to produce a list of aims and objectives. These should answer the following questions.

- What do you want to get out of the group?

- What do you hope to achieve?

- How are you going to work together to achieve this outcome?

Again, if a group member is not pulling their weight, a gentle reminder about the aims and objectives should help.

Producing group assignments

If you have to produce a piece of assessed work, make sure that everyone is clear about the completion date or deadline. Divide the work among group members and make sure that everyone knows what they have to do and when it has to be completed.

It might be useful to consider the strengths and weaknesses of each member; for example, some will be good at research, others good at writing reports. Tasks can be allocated accordingly, which will help motivation levels and improve the success of the group. More information about undertaking project work in groups is provided in Chapter 16.

Tip   Arrange regular meetings to keep track of what everyone is doing. If a group member is not doing their work, the problems can be detected and rectified quickly.

Understanding group roles

People have different roles within a group. The role that each person adopts depends on a number of factors. These can include the purpose of the group, personal characteristics, previous group experience, confidence, knowledge and existing friendships.

For a group to work successfully you need to ensure that all members adopt a positive role. The types of positive role that can be adopted include:

- organizer/planner;
- co-ordinator;
- contributor of information/knowledge;
- researcher;
- mediator/peace-keeper (in particular, if there are some problems between specific group members);
- generator of ideas;
- motivator;
- doer/worker;
- overseer.

If you have members of a group that adopt some or all of these roles, you will find that your group works effectively. However, there are negative roles that people can adopt within a group, and if these are adopted your groupwork will not be so effective. These negative roles can include:

- aggressor;
- disruptor;
- dominator;
- competitor;
- joker/jester;
- non-contributor.

A great deal has been written about group and team roles and, if this is an area that interests you, more information is provided at the end of this chapter.

Recognizing effective and ineffective groups

As we have seen, the roles that people adopt in a group can have an influence on how successful the group is. If your group is dominated by people who have adopted negative roles, it is unlikely that your groupwork will be successful. If this is the case, you need to recognize what roles have been adopted, try to establish why and then attempt to turn the roles from negative to positive (see quotation on the next page). You will find this easier to do if you work through the following stages.

Stage 1

The first stage of this process is to discuss individual roles within the group and to find out what people think about being part of the group. If members are unhappy, they need to be able to talk about the issues, without judgement from others. However, this discussion will need to be chaired, co-ordinated or moderated by someone who is able to make sure that the discussion does not turn to personal insults or attacks on specific group members.

Stage 2

The second stage of the process is to discuss the group outcomes. What is required of the group, and what must be done to make sure that this happens? What positive roles need to be adopted to make sure that all the work is completed successfully? Developing a code of conduct should help members of the group understand what is expected of them in terms of behaviour within the group (see above).

Stage 3

The third stage of the process is to determine whether there are any members within the group who are still disrupting the work. If this is the case, you need to know how to deal with them (see below).

> *'It was a nightmare. He kept making jokes all the time, you know, silly jokes that weren't even funny...it was so hard to work in that group...I think he was insecure or something. So I told him and said we wouldn't get anywhere...yes, others were happy I'd done it...'cos the work counted towards our marks, you know, so it was like, really important. I don't think he knew he was doing it until I said something. Then he stopped doing it and knuckled down.'*
>
> Geoff, Sheffield College

Coping with difficult group members

Every person in your group is different. They all have different personalities, different learning styles and different reasons for enrolling on the course. Despite this, everyone in your group is on your course and therefore has a common bond, which means that most group members are interested in the subject and most will want to do well.

However, there may be exceptions to this rule, and if you find that you are unlucky enough to have an unmotivated, disruptive member in your group, it can create trouble for the rest of you. The following points may help you to resolve problems in your group.

▦ Refer back to the code of conduct and ask that everyone adheres to its rules.

▦ Talk about the situation as soon as it occurs. Don't let problems escalate.

- It is perfectly acceptable to agree to disagree. If someone is adamant about an issue and the work of the group is not moving forward, it might be better to leave the issue and move on to something else.

- If the group member is very disruptive and you can't solve the problems in your group, seek advice from your tutor. You can do this without mentioning names, although your tutor will probably know who you are talking about.

Enhancing your group experience

Groupwork can be a valuable and rewarding experience. To make sure that you get the most out of your groupwork, consider the following points.

- Develop a positive attitude towards groupwork.

- Be prepared to contribute and give your best.

- Get rid of prior expectations about group members.

- Don't get involved in gossip, take sides or be tempted to join factions.

- Recognize that everyone has different knowledge, skills and experiences. Don't be judgemental about these abilities.

- Keep an open mind and try to turn negative experiences into positive. What have you learned and how has it helped you to grow as a student?

Tip You will find your groupwork more rewarding if you are able to recognize the valuable teamwork skills and experience you have developed from your groupwork. This could include communication skills, listening skills, negotiation, co-operation, delegation and conflict resolution.

Summary

Groupwork is an important part of many courses at college and university. To get the most out of your groupwork you need to improve your communication skills and understand what roles are adopted by different members of the group. Some of the roles are positive, whereas others are negative. For a group to work successfully, you need most or all members to adopt positive roles. If a member persists in disrupting the group, you should speak to them or seek further advice from your tutor.

Some courses require students to work in groups on a particular project, whereas others require students to complete projects on their own. There are a number of issues involved in project work, and these are discussed in the following chapter.

Further reading

Belbin, M., *Team Roles at Work*, 2nd edition (Oxford: Butterworth-Heinemann, 2010).

Levin, P., *Successful Teamwork! For undergraduates and taught postgraduates working on group projects* (Maidenhead: Open University Press, 2004).

16 Undertaking projects

Project work is used as a teaching and learning tool in schools, colleges and universities. Projects can be undertaken in groups or on an individual basis and the aim is to encourage independence, imagination, initiative, self-discipline, self-expression, co-operation and the development of research skills. Issues involved in project work at all levels are discussed in this chapter.

Knowing about the different types of project work

There are various types of project that students can undertake, depending on the level of their course, the subject and the teaching preferences of the tutor. Examples of the type of project work that you may be required to undertake include the following.

- Projects that stimulate imagination. These can be used with schoolchildren, for example, to help them to work with others and use their combined powers of imagination to develop something interesting, creative and exciting.

- Projects that require students to find specific information. This type of project can be used at all levels and requires students to search for information, independently of their teacher or tutor. It may require the presentation of specific facts and figures.

- Projects that are related to work and/or vocational aspirations. This type of project can be used at college or university to help students gain experience of practical problems or situations that are relevant to future careers (see example, below).

- Learner-centred projects where the content and presentation are determined by the learners. These can be used at all levels and in all subject areas.

- Project work that requires learners to test theories that they have learned in the classroom. This involves practical work such as experiments and interviewing people.

The Department of Civil Engineering at the University of Bristol brings the design process to life through a series of group projects. One of these projects is to design a water supply system in mid-Wales, based on maps and rainfall data. The project takes place over two weeks and is made as realistic as possible by simulating the atmosphere of a busy design office. Students are required to make a presentation at the end of their project.

Planning your project

Preparation is the key to successful projects. You need to make sure that you understand exactly what is required. Make sure that you have to hand all the equipment you will require and the necessary access to resources. This could include:

- stationery;
- reference books;

- journal articles;
- access to the internet;
- access to a laboratory and equipment;
- access to relevant research participants (see Chapter 17 for more information about conducting interviews and designing questionnaires);
- recording equipment (see Chapter 7);
- data analysis software and/or databases and spreadsheets (see Chapter 12);
- presentation equipment, which could include flip charts, PowerPoint, whiteboards, printers and paper (see Chapter 21).

Brainstorming

When planning your project you need to interpret the objectives and work out how you are going to meet them. Brainstorm your options/ideas in a group or on an individual basis. Brainstorming requires you to think of ideas and write them down, without judgement or evaluation (see Chapter 8). Once you have a list of options/ideas, you can go through each in more detail, deciding which are workable and which should be deleted.

Structuring your project

Once you have made a decision about what is to be included in your project, you need to work out how it is to be completed. Draw up a timetable of what needs to be done and the date by when it should be finished. If you are working in a group you can allocate roles and make sure that everyone knows what they have to do and when it has to be done by (see Chapter 15).

Once the background information has been gathered you can have another brainstorming session to decide how you are going to use the information. Again, after this stage you will be able to work out what information should be included and what should be omitted.

Structuring your work for presentation

When you think about the structure of your project you need to start making decisions about how you are going to present your work, as this will influence the structure. For example, if you are required to produce a written report, you will need to make sure that you have enough information to include in each section of the report.

Although your project can be presented in a variety of ways, in most cases you will need to make sure that you include the following when structuring your project (a more detailed structure for written reports is provided in Chapter 18).

Introduction

What is your project?

Why is it important?

What are your aims and objectives?

What is the background to your project?

Methods

How did you carry out the project work?

What was the timescale?

Who was involved?

Did you encounter any problems?

Is there anything you would improve upon if you were to continue with the project?

Findings/outcome

What have you found out?

What have you produced as a result of your project work? This could include pictures, diagrams, charts, tables, figures, written reports, oral presentations, etc.

Conclusions/summary

What conclusions can be drawn from your project work?

What have you learned? This could include your actual findings and skills that you have gained from undertaking project work.

Managing your project

If you are working in a group it might be prudent to allocate a management role to someone who is able to oversee the work and ensure that each part of the project is completed on time. Make sure that this person is happy in the role and that they are able to motivate other members of the group without antagonizing them (see Chapter 15).

If you are working on your own, consult Chapter 2 for information about time management and planning your work.

Presenting your work

If you have been given the freedom to present your project using a method of your choosing, try to be imaginative and creative in your presentation methods (see quotation opposite).

This will show initiative, add interest and can help you to receive higher marks, if your presentation is executed well.

> *'We went to Carlisle on a geography field trip. We were told to do some research on a topic of our choosing and present our findings to the rest of the group. When we were doing our field work we found, very surprisingly, that Carlisle, at the time, had the worst heroin problem in the country. So we decided to look at this issue and the project sort of changed into something about deprivation.*
>
> *But instead of just presenting the facts and figures, we decided to do a bus tour of Carlisle. So we had to get a map that we could hang up in front of us, then set all the seats up in the form of a bus. All the other students and the tutor had to get on the "bus". One of us was the driver, one the conductor and one the tour guide. We "drove" around the neighbourhoods, pointing out places of interest and relating them to the facts and figures we had found.*
>
> *We got very good marks for our project and other students seemed to enjoy it. It was good for me because I don't like speaking in public, so I was the driver!'*
>
> Elaine, Geography field trip to Carlisle

More information about making oral presentations is provided in Chapter 21 and more information about producing written reports is provided in Chapter 18.

Working on your own

If you are to undertake your project work on your own, you need to maintain high levels of motivation so that you can complete your work successfully. To do this you should make sure that you choose a project that is of personal interest to you. Discuss the available options with your tutor to make sure that you are both happy with the subject.

Information about undertaking independent study is provided in Chapter 9, and this includes comprehensive information about remaining motivated while working independently. If your project work involves an element of primary research (the study of a subject through firsthand observation and investigation) more information is provided in Chapter 17).

Tip Make sure that the topic of your project is relevant to the course and that it will meet the required standards for assessment. If in doubt, discuss the topic with your tutor.

Working with other students

Many courses require project work to be undertaken by groups of students as it encourages co-operation, delegation, negotiation and teamwork. It also enables students to bounce ideas off each other and plan a project that is imaginative and creative.

Group project work can be enjoyable and students often learn more from working in groups than they do from working on their own. This is because people bring different strengths, skills and knowledge to a group and students can learn from each other. However, working with others can be problematic, in particular, in cases where students don't have the same work ethic and where project work is assessed.

Working together successfully

Advice and guidance about working in groups and dealing with disruptive group members are provided in Chapter 15. In addition to this advice, you will find your project work more enjoyable and successful if you take note of the following.

- Develop a team spirit. Get to know each other (which could include socializing together). Support each other and ensure that all members feel part of the team.

- Interaction within a group should be based on mutual respect and encouragement. Listen to all ideas and don't disrespect the views of others.

- Avoid blaming specific people for problems. Instead, look for creative solutions to problems.

- Ideas are important. Concentrate on these rather than individual personalities.

Tip Make sure that you have enough time at the end of your project for all group members to read through the work and/or check the presentation, so that everyone is happy and understands what has been written or what is to be said. Ensure that all mistakes and inaccuracies are ironed out.

Summary

Project work is utilized as a teaching and learning resource on various courses in schools, colleges and universities. Through undertaking project work students are able to develop a variety of skills that will be useful to them in their future lives and careers. When undertaking projects it is important to plan carefully, structure the work, allocate roles, manage the project and present the findings in a way that is suitable for the subject and level of the course.

For some projects you will need to conduct your own social research. Guidance on how to do this is offered in the following chapter.

17 **Conducting social research**

As a social science or humanities student you may have to conduct primary research as part of your coursework. This involves the study of a subject through firsthand observation and investigation, which may include research methods such as interviews, focus groups and questionnaires.

When conducting social research it is important to plan your work carefully as this will help you to avoid mistakes later in your work, and will ensure that you collect the type of data that is relevant to your topic. It is also important to understand which research methods are the most appropriate for your topic and know how to analyse your data. These issues are discussed in this chapter.

Beginning a research project

When you start to think about your research project you need to work through the five 'Ws'.

1. What is your research? This is a very important starting point. If you are able to define your topic succinctly, you will find it easier to carry out the research.
2. Why do you want to do the research? Think very carefully about this as it affects your topic, the way you conduct the research and the way that you report the results.

3. Who are the research subjects or participants? Do you need to specify how many people you should contact?

4. Where are you going to conduct your research? Do you have the resources and time available to travel any distance, or do you need to conduct the work closer to college/university or home? If you are gong to conduct interviews or focus groups, where will you hold them?

5. When are you going to do your research? Is your proposed research possible in the time that you have available? Will you be able to contact all participants within this timescale?

'When students are deciding on a topic for their dissertation I ask them to think about what they want to do, why they want to do it and then how they intend to do it. They must also work out whether their proposed research will enable them to produce work of the required intellectual standard. They must make sure that there is enough material to write a dissertation of 10,000 words. Sometimes their proposed research would generate far too much information, and sometimes it's not enough.'

Dave, Sheffield Hallam University

Choosing a research methodology

Once you have answered the five 'Ws' you can go on to think about how you are going to do your research. First, you need to think about your research methodology. This is the philosophy or the general principle that will guide your research. It is the overall approach to studying your topic and includes issues that you need to think about such as the constraints, dilemmas and ethical choices within your research.

Tip Your research methodology differs from your research methods (these are the tools that you use to gather data, such as questionnaires or interviews).

Qualitative and quantitative research

When you start to think about your research methodology, you need to consider the differences between qualitative and quantitative research.

Qualitative research

Qualitative research explores attitudes, behaviour and experiences through methods such as interviews or focus groups. It attempts to get an in-depth opinion from participants. As it is attitudes, behaviour and experiences that are important, fewer people take part in the research, but the contact with these people tends to last a lot longer.

Quantitative research

Quantitative research generates statistics through the use of large-scale survey research, using methods such as questionnaires or structured interviews. This type of research reaches many more people, but the contact with those people is much quicker than it is in qualitative research.

Choosing research methods

Once you have thought about your research methodology, you can go on to consider the research methods that you are going to use to gather your data. The following points will help with your choices.

- Your choice of research methodology will have a big influence on your choice of methods. Qualitative methodologies suggest methods such as unstructured or semi-structured interviews, focus groups and open-ended questionnaires. Quantitative methodologies suggest closed-ended questionnaires or structured interviews that generate statistics (see page 166).

- When deciding on your methods, think about the purpose of your research. If it is to generate statistics you need a method that will do this, such as a closed-ended questionnaire. If is to generate a detailed description a method such as unstructured or semi-structured interviews would be appropriate (see page 168).

- It is not necessary to use only one research method, although many projects do this. A combination of methods can be desirable as it enables you to overcome the weaknesses inherent in different methods.

- In quantitative research you are able to define your research methods early in the planning stage. You know what you want to find out and you can decide on the best way to obtain the information. Also, you can decide how many people you need to contact in the planning stages.

- For some types of qualitative research it may be difficult to decide on all your methods at the beginning of a project or know how many people you need to contact. It is also possible for your methods to change as your research progresses.

- When deciding on your methods you must be aware of the constraints under which you will have to work; for example, your timescale, budget and available resources.

The three most common research methods used by students in the social sciences and humanities are questionnaires, interviews and focus groups. These are discussed below. However, there are other methods that can be used and if you are interested in any of these, useful publications are listed at the end of the chapter.

Using questionnaires

There are three basic types of questionnaire: closed-ended, open-ended or a combination of both.

▪ Closed-ended questionnaires are used to generate statistics in quantitative research. As these questionnaires follow a set format, and as most can be scanned straight into a computer for ease of analysis, greater numbers can be produced.

▪ Open-ended questionnaires are used in qualitative research, although some researchers will quantify the answers during the analysis stage. The questionnaire does not contain boxes to tick, but instead leaves a blank section for the respondent to write in an answer. As there are no standard answers to these questions, data analysis is more complex. Also, as it is opinions that are sought rather than numbers, fewer questionnaires need to be distributed.

▪ Combination questionnaires are used by researchers when they want to generate statistics and find out about ideas, beliefs and/or experiences. The questionnaire contains a mix of questions, some with boxes to tick and some with spaces for longer answers.

For information about how to construct questionnaires, see Table 4.

Table 4. Constructing questionnaires.

Wording	Design
Questions should be kept short and simple	Questionnaires must be relevant to the lives, attitudes and beliefs of the respondents
Questions should be easy to understand	Make the questionnaire interesting

Wording	Design
Questions need to be clear and unambiguous	Keep the questionnaire as short as possible
Avoid jargon and technical terms	Start with easy-to-answer questions
Avoid words that have double meanings	Group the questions into specific topics
Don't use questions that will cause annoyance, frustration, offence, embarrassment or sadness	Use filter questions to enable respondents to skip questions that aren't relevant to them
Avoid emotive words	Make sure the questionnaire is not too cluttered
Avoid leading questions	Include plenty of white space
Don't use double-barrelled questions (two questions in one)	Leave enough space for answers (open-ended)
Avoid negative questions	Make sure all possible answers are covered (closed-ended)

Administering questionnaires

Questionnaires can be researcher-administered (the researcher/student asks the questions and writes in the answers) or self-administered (the respondent reads the questions and writes in the answers). They can be distributed online, via the post or in person.

Piloting questionnaires

All questionnaires must be piloted (tested). This is extremely important as it helps you to work out which questions are unclear or badly worded and shows you whether your questionnaire will generate the type of information that you are hoping for.

Test the questionnaire on the type of people who will be taking part in the main survey. Make sure that they know it is a pilot test and ask them to forward any comments they may have about the topic, length, structure and wording.

Go through each response very carefully, noting comments and analysing answers as this will help you to discover whether there are ambiguities present. Alter the questionnaire, if required.

Tip If you have had to undertake major alterations as a result of your pilot, you may need to pilot the questionnaire again.

Interviewing people

The most common types of interview used in social research are unstructured, semi-structured and structured interviews.

Unstructured interviews

Unstructured or in-depth interviews are sometimes called life history interviews. In this type of interview, the researcher attempts to achieve a holistic understanding of the interviewee's point of view or situation. The participant is free to talk about what he or she deems important, with little directional influence from the researcher. Unstructured interviews can be used only for qualitative research and produce a great deal of data that can be difficult to analyse.

Semi-structured interviews

Semi-structured interviewing is perhaps the most common type of interview used in qualitative social research. In this type of interview, the researcher wants to know specific information that can be compared and contrasted with information gained in other interviews. To do this, the same questions need to be asked in each interview. However, the researcher also wants the interview to remain flexible so that other important issues can still arise, hence the term 'semi-structured'.

Structured interviews

Structured interviews are used in quantitative research and can be conducted face-to-face, over the telephone or online. This interview technique is highly structured and the respondent can't answer questions in any other way than the answers that are provided on the form. This means that, to avoid frustrating respondents and invalidating results, the list of answers should cover all possible responses.

Tip When conducting interviews you need to dress and behave appropriately. This will help you to establish rapport with the interviewee.

Conducting focus groups

Focus groups are also called discussion groups or group interviews. With this method a number of people are asked to come together to discuss a certain issue. The discussion is led by a moderator who introduces the topic, asks questions, controls digressions and stops breakaway conversations. Focus groups can be video-recorded or tape-recorded.

If you intend to use focus groups in your research, you should take note of the following.

▪ Choose your participants carefully. Your aim is a free-flowing discussion, so your participants must feel comfortable in each other's company and be able to talk to each other about the topic.

▪ The ideal number is nine or eleven (odd numbers work better than even numbers because it is harder for people to pair up into break-away conversations).

▪ The venue needs to be a quiet room free from noise, disturbances and distractions.

▪ You need a good-quality audio or video recorder that has been thoroughly tested. It should be placed on a non-vibratory surface, in the centre of the group, away from background noises.

▪ As the facilitator/moderator you will need to be aware of group dynamics and know how to control breakaway conversations, digressions and disruptive group members. See *Introduction to Research Methods* (details in Further reading) for information about how to do this effectively. More information about group dynamics is provided in Chapter 15.

Tip When conducting focus groups you will need to discuss issues of anonymity, confidentiality and personal disclosure before the discussion begins.

Analysing data

The methods that you use to analyse your data will depend on whether you have chosen to conduct quantitative or qualitative research.

Quantitative data analysis

For quantitative data analysis, issues of validity and reliability are important. Quantitative researchers endeavour to show that their chosen methods succeed in measuring what they purport to measure. They want to make sure that their measurements are stable and consistent and that there are no errors or bias present, either from the respondents or from the researcher.

For quantitative data, the analysis is left until the end of the data collection process and, if it is a large survey, statistical software is the easiest and most efficient method to use. Analysis is quick and efficient, with most software packages producing well-presented graphs, pie charts and tables that can be used for your final report.

More information about statistics is provided in Chapter 11 and comprehensive information about analysing quantitative data can be found in some of the publications listed on the next page.

Qualitative data analysis

Qualitative data analysis is a very personal process, with few rigid rules and procedures. There are many different types of qualitative data analysis and the method that you use will depend on your research topic, your personal preferences and the time, equipment and finances available to you.

Often in qualitative data analysis the researcher analyses as the research progresses, continually refining and reorganizing in light of the emerging results. This analysis helps the researcher to decide where and how they wish to collect their next data.

If you are interested in finding out more about qualitative data analysis, see Further reading, on the next page.

Tip To analyse qualitative data you need to produce the information in a way that can be analysed. This might be interview transcripts, a series of written answers on an open-ended questionnaire, field notes or memos, for example.

Summary

Most social science and humanities students will need to conduct some primary research as part of their studies, usually for extended projects or for their dissertation. When conducting primary research, decisions have to be made about the research methodology and the research methods. The topic and purpose of the research will help you to make your choice and tutors will be able to offer further advice and guidance.

Once you have conducted your primary research and analysed the results, you need to write up your research report or dissertation. Information on how to do this is provided in the following chapter.

Further reading

Creswell, J.W., *Research Design: Qualitative, quantitative, and mixed methods approaches*, 3rd edition (Thousand Oaks, CA: Sage, 2008).

Dawson, C., *Introduction to Research Methods*, 4th edition (Oxford: How To Books, 2009).

Hahn, C., *Doing Qualitative Research Using Your Computer: A practical guide* (London: Sage, 2009).

Hardy, M. and Bryman, A. (eds), *Handbook of Data Analysis* (London: Sage, 2009).

18 Writing a long report or dissertation

Students studying on undergraduate or higher-level further education courses, in most cases, will need to write a long report or dissertation, based on their primary research. To be successful in this you need to pay close attention to structure and style, understand how to use and present data, know how to present your work and produce a convincing bibliography. These issues are discussed in this chapter.

Knowing about structure and style

If you have to write a long report or a dissertation you should ask your tutor about whether there are structural guidelines specific to your course or collge/university that you should follow. If not, the generally accepted format for long reports and dissertations is as follows.

Title page

This contains the title of the dissertation/report, the name of the student and the date of completion. It includes details about the purpose of the dissertation/report. For example: 'A dissertation submitted in partial fulfilment of the requirements of Kent University for the degree of BA Honours Combined Humanities'.

Contents page

This section lists the contents of the report/dissertation, either in chapter or section headings with subheadings, and their page numbers.

List of illustrations/tables

This section includes the title and page numbers of all graphs, tables, illustrations, charts and diagrams.

Acknowledgements

Some students may wish to acknowledge the help of their research participants, tutors, employers and/or funding body, if relevant.

Abstract/summary

This is a short summary of the research, its purpose, methods, main findings and conclusion. If your report is orientated towards business, this section could instead give a list of practical recommendations based on the results of your research.

Introduction

This section introduces the research, setting out the aims and objectives, terms and definitions. It includes a rationale for the research and a summary of the dissertation/report structure.

Background

This section includes all your background research, which can be obtained from the literature, from personal experience or both. All sources of information must be acknowledged if you are to avoid accusations of plagiarism, so you must keep careful records from the beginning of your research (see Chapters 3 and 6).

Research methodology and methods

This section provides a description of, and justification for, your chosen research methodology and methods. It should include all the practical information that examiners will need to evaluate your work; for example, how many people took part, how they were chosen, your timescale and data recording and analysis methods.

Findings/analysis

This section is the heart of your report/dissertation and includes your main findings. The content will depend on your chosen methodology and methods. For example, if you have conducted a large quantitative survey, this section may contain tables, graphs, pie charts and associated statistics. If you have conducted a qualitative piece of research, this section may consist of descriptive prose containing carefully selected quotations.

Conclusion

This section sums up your findings and draws conclusions from them, perhaps in relation to other research or literature.

Further research

This section illustrates the ways in which your research could be continued. For example, you could make suggestions about how your research could be expanded upon in cases where results are inconclusive or where your research has generated more questions that need to be addressed.

References

This section includes all the literature that you have referred to, specifically, in your report/dissertation.

Bibliography

If you have read other books in relation to your research but have not referred to them specifically when writing up your report/dissertation, you should include them in a bibliography. However, you must make sure that the references are relevant to your work and that you have really read them. Adding references to pad out your bibliography is a tactic frowned upon by examiners.

Appendices

If you have constructed a questionnaire for your research, or produced an interview schedule or a code of ethics, it may be useful to include them in your report as an appendix. You can also include charts, graphs and tables as an appendix.

In general, appendices don't count towards your total amount of words so it is a useful way to include material without taking up valuable space. However, make sure that you don't fill up your report with irrelevant appendices as this will not impress examiners.

Tip When including material in your report you must make sure that it is relevant. Ask yourself whether the examiner will gain a deeper understanding of your work by reading the information and, if not, leave it out.

Using statistics, facts, opinions and arguments

When you write a report or dissertation you may need to include statistics, facts, arguments and opinions that have been generated by yourself or other researchers. When including this type of information, you need to be aware of the difference between each of these. You also need to know how to critique and analyse statistics, facts, opinions and arguments to help you make judgements about the validity and reliability of the information you are presenting.

Statistics

Statistics is a numerical discipline that involves collecting, organizing, analysing, interpreting and presenting data. We also refer to the data that is presented as statistics. The data is only as good as the methods used to create it and the skill of the statistician who collects the data. Figures can be misleading, incorrect (whether deliberate or by mistake) and open to misinterpretation. It is important to analyse all statistics carefully before including them in your report.

Facts

Facts are things that can be investigated and are found to be true. They tend to be exact and specific. However, not everything presented as a 'fact' is correct and true, so again, you need to check your sources and make sure that the information is valid and reliable before presenting the facts in your report.

Opinions

Opinions are personal beliefs or judgements that are not based on proof or certainty. When presenting opinions in your work, you need to make this clear, by stating 'in my opinion', or 'in the opinion of…'. It is fine to use opinions in your work if they help to move your discussion forward, but you must acknowledge that they are opinions, rather than facts.

Arguments

Arguments are reasons or explanations given to support or reject a view. In your written work arguments are used to prove something through using reason and supporting evidence, which can be facts, statistics and the arguments of experts in the field (these must be acknowledged). It is up to you to demonstrate that the arguments you are using can be backed up by the evidence.

More information about critiquing and reviewing is provided in Chapter 8 and more information about using statistics is provided in Chapter 11.

> *'Unfortunately many social science students just don't understand statistics and we often find that their use of statistics is rubbish. It really frustrates me. We try to address the problem by providing a statistics module, but many students just don't register for it because they perceive it to be too complicated. But if they want to understand the statistics they are quoting or producing, they should do that course.'*
>
> Dave, Sheffield Hallam University

Using personal experiences

Personal experience can be a valuable background tool and can help you to focus in on a research topic that is of particular interest and relevance to your life. When you write your report/dissertation it is possible to describe these experiences and how they relate to your work.

However, when doing this, you should take note of the following.

- Check with your tutor as to whether it is acceptable to use personal experience when writing your report/dissertation. Some subjects/tutors may discourage this practice.
- Make it clear that you are writing about personal experience.
- Don't ramble. It can be very easy to get carried away with long descriptions about what has happened in the past.
- Keep descriptions of personal experience short and to the point. They must be relevant to your research.
- Avoid anecdotes and emotion. Academic writing needs to show reason and logic and should be backed up with evidence. Even if your personal experience provides some evidence, you should try to back up your arguments with evidence from other sources.

Presenting data

When presenting data in your written work you need to choose the most appropriate method that will display your data clearly and succinctly. The most common methods are diagrams, tables, charts and graphs (see Chapters 10 and 11).

When presenting your data in your report you should take note of the following.

- Make sure that all diagrams, charts, tables and graphs are titled and have a number. The title, number and page number should be included in the list of illustrations at the beginning of your report (see above). All columns, bars and axes must also be labelled clearly.

- All illustrations/figures must be relevant to your writing, and must be referred to, and discussed, in your text. Don't leave illustrations and figures to speak for themselves.

- The general rule is that all illustrations/figures that are essential to your explanation should be included within the main body of the text, whereas illustrations and figures that are supportive of your explanation can be included in an appendix at the end of your report (see page 176).

- Illustrations/figures that you are using from somebody else's work must be clearly labelled and the source acknowledged, including title, author, year and page number.

Tip   Check all your figures carefully. Ensure sure that they add up and make sense. You might find it useful to ask a friend to check the figures for you.

Editing and proofreading

Once you have completed a draft of your report/dissertation, you must edit your work. When doing so, consider the following points.

- Make sure that your report is of the required length.

- Check sentence structure, grammar and punctuation. Make sure that sentences and paragraphs are not too long and that they flow on from one to the next.

- Make sure that your introduction introduces the work, that the main body discusses your findings and your conclusions sum up your work. Check that each section flows into the next.

- Check all figures, charts, tables, graphs and diagrams. Make sure that they are labelled correctly, that all figures are correct and that you have discussed each illustration within the text.

- Check for irrelevant material, digressions, generalizations, assumptions and misleading data or assertions. Rewrite or delete any problem areas.

You may need to edit your work several times until you are happy with the content and structure. Once you have done this, you can go on to proofread your work. More information about editing and proofreading is provided in Chapter 5.

Presenting your work

Your college/university will have strict rules about how your work should be presented, so you must make sure that you follow their guidelines. Ask your tutor for guidance.

Most institutions have a binding department. Members of staff will make sure that your work is bound in the correct way, for a small fee. You should ensure that you produce the work in the required manner, paying attention to size of margin and page layout. If using your own printer, set it to high quality, use good-quality paper and print only on one side of A4 paper.

Oral presentations

In some cases you may need to make an oral presentation, in addition to producing your written report. If this is the case you should speak to your tutor to find out what is required. More information about making an oral presentation is provided in Chapter 21.

Producing references and a bibliography

At this stage of your course you should know what referencing system is used by your college/university. If not, speak to your tutor.

A popular method is the Harvard system. This lists the authors' surnames alphabetically, followed by their initials, date of publication, title of book in italics, place of publication and publisher. If the reference is a journal article, the title of the article appears in inverted commas and the name of the journal appears in italics, followed by the volume number and pages of the article. A sample reference section from a undergraduate dissertation is provided in the box below.

Sample reference section from an undergraduate dissertation

Cohen, A.P. (1994) *Self Consciousness: An alternative anthropology of identity*, London: Routledge.

Cook, J.A. and Fonow, M.M. (1986) 'Knowledge and Women's Interests: Issues of epistemology and methodology in feminist sociological research', *Sociological Enquiry*, 56: 2–29.

Currie, D. and Kazi, H. (1987) 'Academic Feminism and the Process of De-radicalisation: Re-examining the issues', *Feminist Review*, 25: 77–98.

Faludi, S. (1992) *Backlash: The undeclared war against women*, London: Chatto and Windus.

More information about referencing, including referencing online sources, is provided in Chapter 6.

Using bibliographic software

There is a variety of bibliographic software packages available on the market. Some of these are free and open-source, whereas others have a hefty price tag. Examples include:

- Scholar's Aid (www.scholarsaid.com);
- RefWorks (www.refworks.com);
- EndNote (www.endnote.com);
- Reference Manager (www.refman.com);
- ProCite (www.procite.com).

These packages enable you to create, store, search and constantly update your personal library of references, and are extremely useful when it comes to producing a reference and a bibliography for your report/dissertation. The software is also useful for helping you to summarize useful references (your summary is searchable so that you can find articles, even if you can't remember the author or title). You can save PDFs of useful articles and links to relevant websites.

Contact your college/university IT services to find out which packages are available for your use or visit the websites listed above for more information about specification and prices.

Improving your marks

You can improve your report/dissertation marks by taking notice of the following.

- The topic must be relevant to your course.
- The research should be unique or offer a new insight or development.

- The title, aims and objectives should be clear and succinct.

- Your background research should be thorough, comprehensive and well referenced.

- Your research methods should be suitable for your chosen topic.

- You should critique methods that did not work as planned.

- The report should be of the right length, well written, well structured, well presented and free from mistakes.

- Your arguments must be convincing and well thought out.

- Your conclusion should be interesting and must provide a good summary of the research.

Summary

When writing a long report or a dissertation it should be produced in the correct manner, to a high standard and be of the required length. You must pay close attention to style and structure and ensure that there are no grammatical or spelling mistakes. All arguments should be well presented and backed up with relevant evidence. Opinions and personal experience should be acknowledged.

Long reports and/or dissertations are assessed and count towards your final course marks. Another method of assessment is the traditional examination, and these are discussed in the following chapter.

Further reading

Swetnam, D., *Writing Your Dissertation: The bestselling guide to planning, preparing and presenting first-class work*, 3rd edition, revised and updated (Oxford: How To Books Ltd, 2004).

19 Passing examinations

Examinations are used to test students' knowledge, understanding and/or skill. They can involve written tests, oral questions or practical tests, depending on the type of course, assessment procedures and preferences of the tutor.

This chapter discusses the traditional written examination, and includes information about how to revise, how to take an exam and how to improve marks. Chapter 20 goes on to provide information about taking other types of test.

Revising effectively

'Revise' means to re-read, review and organize information so that you are able to understand what you have been taught and commit the information to memory. To revise effectively you should carry out systematic revision throughout your course. If you do this, rather than cramming in all your revision before your exams, you will find it easier to commit information to memory and your understanding of the course material will improve.

When revising, you need to revise lecture notes, seminar papers, assignments, handouts, books, podcasts, journal articles and any other information that is relevant to your course syllabus.

Revising for examinations

Your examination revision will be more effective if you take note of the following.

- Start your examination revision 6–10 weeks before your exams begin.

- Draw up a revision plan/timetable. This should include:
  - dates of all your exams;
  - a list of all your examination subjects and an estimation of how much time you will need to revise each one;
  - a specific plan for each week.

- Use revision checklists or your course syllabus to check that you have all the information you require. If you have gaps in your knowledge, return to your notes, library or the internet. However, make sure that you only read around subjects that are included in the syllabus.

- Obtain copies of previous exam papers from your tutor or college/university intranet/VLE. Take note of the number, length, structure, level and wording of questions. Remember that the syllabus might have changed, so don't worry if different subjects appear on old papers.

- Attend an examination session, if possible. This will cover issues such as what to expect during the exam, rules and regulations, revision techniques and information about the number and type of questions (see quotation on the next page). If your tutor doesn't hold this type of session, find out whether a session is run by your department or the study support unit (see Appendix 2).

- Revise in short bursts and take a short break every hour. Try to do a little every day.

■ Break down subjects into specific topics and revise two or three of these in more depth. You should be able to answer questions on these topics, which will help you to be more relaxed and confident.

'I use one of the last sessions of the course to talk about exams. I give the students a revision checklist and a copy of the course syllabus. I stress that only those subjects will be included in the exam. Then I give them a list of things that can be taken into exams, and the procedures that have to be adopted. I'll also give them information about where exams are to be held. If we have time we'll try answering a question in the twenty minutes that students have. It's useful for students because a lot of them aren't used to writing so quickly with pen and paper.'

Anne, Bournemouth University

Using online revision tools

There are various online revision tools available for students studying at all levels on all types of course. These tools can help you to prepare a revision timetable, write revision notes, make revision cards and share resources with fellow students. If you are interested in using any of these tools, the following websites are good places to start.

■ www.revisionworld.co.uk (for GCSE and A Level students);

■ http://getrevising.co.uk (all levels and qualifications);

■ www.bbc.co.uk/schools/bitesize (for GCSE and A Level students).

In addition to these online learning tools there is a comprehensive, free, online revision and examination unit provided by the Open University called 'Revision and examinations'. Visit http://openlearn.open.ac.uk to access this course. The unit should take six hours to complete and is useful for students studying at college and university.

'I encourage my students to form revision groups. You can brain-storm exam questions, share assignments, swap revision tips, encourage and support each other, try mock questions and bounce ideas off each other.'

Anne, Bournemouth University

Preparing for an exam

The following list will help with your exam preparation.

- Find out the exact date and time of your exams. Check that there are no clashes and, if there are, inform your tutor or course director immediately.
- Find out where the examination venue is situated. Check car-parking or the proximity of public transport stops, if relevant.
- Ask your tutor about what you can and can't take with you into the examination room. Don't breach the rules.
- Find out what form of identity you need to take and remember to take it with you.
- Find out which pens help you to write the quickest and which are the most comfortable to use. Buy several of these pens and make sure that you take at least two to each exam.

Tip Don't try to cram in any last-minute revision the night before. Instead, try to relax and unwind. Treat yourself to a stress-free evening, if possible.

Taking an exam

Buy a good, reliable alarm clock and make sure that it is set correctly for the day of your exam. Arrive at the venue at least ten minutes before the doors open. If you are late for any reason and are not allowed into the room, you must report to your course office or tutor immediately and explain the reason for being late. At some institutions you may be allowed to re-sit the exam.

Once in the exam hall you should take note of the following.

▪ Don't look at the exam paper until you are told to do so by the invigilator.

▪ When you are told to turn over the paper, read all instructions carefully. Find out how many questions you are expected to answer. Note whether there are any questions that are compulsory. Find out whether you have to answer a certain number of questions from each section.

▪ Work out how much time you have for each question. Note the amount of marks each section is worth, if this information is supplied. Those sections with more marks will require more time to be spent on them.

▪ Read all the questions before you start to write your answers. As you go through them, tick any that you think you could answer.

▪ Check all sides of the exam paper to make sure that you haven't missed any information.

▪ Some institutions will give you reading time before you go on to answer questions. Use this time wisely to make sure that you understand all that is being asked of you. Make some notes as you read the questions.

▪ Answer your best question first as this will help you to relax and feel more confident. It should also be quicker to complete, which will give you more time for the harder questions.

- Write as clearly and as legibly as possible.

- Keep an eye on the time and make sure that you spend only the required time on each answer and then move on. You can always come back to an unfinished answer at the end.

- If you are stuck recollecting a fact or figure, leave a blank space as you might remember later.

- If you find yourself running out of time, jot down the main points you wanted to include in the rest of the answer as some examiners will award additional marks.

'I would advise all students to read recent exam papers and look at what comes up each year. Sometimes the same subjects come up year after year and this gives you a very good clue as to what you should be revising!'

Anne, Bournemouth University

Improving exam marks

The following tips have been provided by tutors who regularly mark examination papers.

- Make sure that you follow the instructions carefully and answer the correct number of questions. If any answers are missing you will not receive any marks and this will bring your average score down.

- Answer all the questions and don't spend too much time on one particular question. Leave a space and return to the question if you have time at the end. Note that you will receive more marks for partial answers than no answer at all.

- Make sure that the answer you provide is relevant to the question. You won't get extra marks for padding out an answer with irrelevant material.

- In mathematical papers always write down the steps you take to work out a problem as you will get marks for these steps, even if your final answer is wrong.

- Write as legibly as possible. Practise with a pen and paper, under mock conditions, and get used to the feel of writing in this way, especially if you're used to producing written work on a PC/laptop. As an examiner I find it extremely frustrating trying to read illegible scripts.

Tip When you have finished an exam, start to think about the next one. Don't spend time worrying about how well or badly you night have performed as it is very hard to tell and can distract you from your revision.

Coping with stress

Good preparation and hard work will help you to feel more confident and relaxed. This, in turn, will help you to cope with examination stress. Increasing your knowledge about the examination process and making sure that you are familiar with the venue and procedures will also help you to cope with nerves.

Most students get nervous about exams. This is perfectly understandable and acceptable. Indeed, this type of heightened awareness often helps us to perform better.

However, some students find that they are consumed by stress and examination fear. If this is the case, speak to your tutor. If you have a serious, recognizable problem, your tutor may be able to make alternative arrangements for you, such as arranging for you to sit the exam on your own, or in a small group. More information about overcoming nerves is provided in Chapter 20.

Summary

Revision is in activity that should take place throughout your course as this will help you to better understand and retain information. When it comes to revising for exams, you should begin in plenty of time and draw up a comprehensive revision timetable. Being well prepared and becoming familiar with exam procedures and venues will help you to relax and feel more confident about taking exams. All exam rules and regulations should be understood and followed.

In addition to the traditional examination described above, you may also be required to take shorter written tests, oral tests, open-book tests, online tests or answer multiple choice questions. These issues are discussed in the following chapter.

20 **Passing tests**

When studying at college and university you may be required to take tests. Some of these tests will count towards your final qualification, whereas others are used to check that you have understood the course so far and to find out whether there are any topics that need further coverage and/or revision.

There are different types of test, depending on your subject, level of course, college/university and the preferences of your tutor. These include written tests, oral tests, open-book tests, online tests and multiple-choice tests. These are discussed below.

Preparing for and taking written tests

There are a variety of written tests that are used by tutors in colleges and universities. The most common type is the traditional examination, discussed in Chapter 19. However, there are other types that may be used on your course. These include tests in which a tutor will read out each question and ask you to write a short answer in a given time, or a questionnaire type test, where you are required to write your answers in the spaces provided.

Tip Tests should never be missed, even if they don't count towards your final mark. They have been developed to help you, and if you miss a test you won't know how well you are progressing and how well you understand the subject.

Revising for written tests

If you know that a written test has been scheduled, you can prepare for the test by revising the topic in depth. Information about how to do this is provided in Chapter 19. Some tests will be on specific topics so you will need to revise only that topic. Your tutor will design the test so that he or she can test your knowledge and understanding of the topic, before moving on to the next topic in lectures/classes.

However, some tests are not scheduled and can be sprung on you at any time during your course (see quotation below). Therefore, it is important that you revise your class/lecture notes, and complete all the background reading, as your course progresses. That way, you will be able to understand and retain more of the information and won't be caught out by unexpected written tests.

> *'Sometimes I prefer not to tell my students that I'm going to test them so I can find out how much they've learned and remembered from the course so far. There's always a groan when I say we're going to have a test, but I try to make them as stress-free as possible and it's so useful to find out how well students are doing. If most of my students get a certain question wrong, I can return to that topic and go over it in more depth.'*
>
> Kate, Weymouth College

Taking written tests

When taking a written test make sure that you read or listen to all the instructions carefully. If you are unclear about any of these instructions, ask your tutor for clarification before the test starts. Ensure that you adhere to all rules and regulations set by your tutor.

Although some written tests tend to be less formal than the traditional examination, you will find the information offered in Chapter 19 useful when taking written tests.

Preparing for and taking oral tests

Oral tests are designed to test your knowledge and under-standing of a subject, along with your oral communication skills. They are used most often on language courses but can be used by tutors on other types of course.

During these tests each student is asked a set of predefined questions and the tutor listens to, and evaluates, answers. The tests can take place on an individual basis, or might take place in front of other students.

The following tips will help you to prepare for and take oral tests.

- Ask you tutor to describe the test procedure and rules and regulations so that you know what to expect.

- Practise the test beforehand. Ask your tutor for some sample questions and practise with another student or anticipate the type of questions that may be asked and practise answering with your partner.

- Find out what you need for the test and make sure that you know where it is to be held. If you are going to use any props or equipment, make sure that they work and that you are familiar with their use.

- Turn up in plenty of time.

- Listen carefully to each question and make sure that you understand what is being asked. If you don't understand the question, or don't hear properly, ask the examiner to repeat the question.

- Maintain good eye contact and posture. Try not to fiddle, fidget or become distracted by anything going on around you.

▪ Once the question has been asked, pause briefly to gather your thoughts and to put some structure into your answer. Don't be afraid of short silences.

▪ Answer the question in a logical way. If you lose your train of thought, ask for the question to be repeated.

▪ If you don't know an answer, don't panic. Try to give the best answer that you can, but don't waffle or ramble on about an unrelated issue.

Tip   If your oral test is timed, have a clock or watch in easy view. Monitor the time and complete your answer within the timescale. If you know the answer well and are confident that you are right, you don't have to spend the whole allotted time, but can indicate that you are ready to move on to the next question.

Preparing for and taking open-book tests

The term 'open-book test' refers to a test or examination into which you are able to take items such as books, handouts, journal articles and notes. Open-book tests are used to test your understanding of a subject, your ability to find information from books or other sources and your skills of synthesis, analysis, judgement and evaluation. Unlike other types of test, they are not used to test your ability to memorize specific information.

The following points will help you to prepare for and take open-book tests.

▪ The key to success is good preparation, excellent organization and familiarity with your subject and the literature. Make sure that you attend all your classes, read around the subject, organize your notes and revise each topic as your course progresses. Keep up to date on current developments within the subject.

▪ Think about all the ideas and concepts that are to be tested (your previous lecture notes should provide a good guide to these). Write a short summary of each and carefully select information that you can take with you to help back up your arguments.

▪ Organize your reference material so that you can find all the information quickly and easily. Mark or highlight important pages. Use book markers, sticky notes, colour coding, written headings or anything else that will help you to locate material quickly.

▪ Check that you have all the required material and arrive at the venue in plenty of time.

▪ Read each question carefully and answer the easiest first. Keep to the point and make sure that you don't use irrelevant material.

▪ Use quotations to back up a point that you are making, but make sure that you keep them short and don't over-quote. Ensure that all quotations are referenced carefully and clearly.

▪ Your personal argument must be clear in your answers.

Tip The items that you are able to take with you vary from course to course, so you must speak to your tutor to ensure that you are absolutely clear about what you can use during the open-book test.

Preparing for and taking online tests

Some tutors may use online tests to help them to test your knowledge and understanding of the course. There is a wide variety of tests that can be used depending on the subject, the level of your course and the preferences of your tutor. The following points will help you when preparing for and taking online tests.

- Revise throughout your course and prior to the test (see Chapter 19).

- Make sure that you are familiar with the technology. Practise beforehand so that you can iron out any problems or speak to your tutor about any problems that are concerning you.

- Understand the instructions and login process, and make sure that you know how to access the test. Some tests will allow you to access them only once, so you must be clear about what you have to do.

- Find out if your online test is 'open-book' (see page 196) and, if so, make sure that you have all the sources to hand before you begin the test.

- If you have to take the test at a specific location, make sure that you know how to find the venue and that you take with you any required identification.

- If you are to take the test at home, make sure that you will not be disturbed as you may not have the chance to pause or save your answers once you have started the test.

- Read all instructions carefully. Note how long the test will take. Find out whether you have to answer the questions in a specific sequence or whether you can save answers, return to them later and alter anything if you think you have got it wrong or want to change your mind. Find out whether you are able to use the back button, or whether this will ruin your test.

- Ensure that you understand how to save and submit answers.

Tip If possible, read through all your answers carefully to make sure that you are happy with them before you submit.

Preparing for and taking multiple-choice tests

Multiple-choice tests and examinations ask students to recognize a correct answer among a set of options that include three or four wrong answers. Students often think that these tests are easier than tests that require them to provide the answers themselves. However, this is not always the case (see below).

Revising for multiple-choice tests

Multiple-choice tests are quick to answer and, therefore, can cover a much broader range of information. This means that you will have to prepare early so that you can commit the required information to memory.

Multiple-choice tests, in many cases, focus on details, and you cannot retain many details effectively in your short-term memory. If you make sure that you learn a small amount each day and allow plenty of time for repeated reviews of the information, you will build a much more reliable long-term memory. More information about short- and long-term memory is provided in Chapter 1 and more information about revising for exams is provided in Chapter 19.

Answering multiple-choice questions

Your multiple-choice tests will be more successful if you take note of the following tips. Although some of these may seem obvious, tutors are often surprised by how many simple points are missed by students when they are placed in a stressful, test-taking environment.

- Read all instructions carefully before you begin. Make sure that you understand how many questions need to be answered and in what time.

- Preview the test. Read through each question quickly, answering all those that you know to be correct.

- Return to the beginning to take more time on those questions that you have not yet answered. If you are still completely baffled, mark the answer you think to be correct in draft, and return later when you have answered as many questions as possible. Don't waste too much time on one question.

- Make sure that you read each question fully and that you understand it completely before choosing an answer.

- Try to answer the question before you look at the given answers.

- Make sure that you read all the possible answers before choosing one.

- Eliminate any answers that you know to be wrong.

- Don't be afraid to change your answers, but don't become distracted by previous answers as you progress in the test.

- If you have time, check through your answers one more time. Since most multiple-choice tests are scanned, you need to make sure that your answers are clear and that all mistakes are erased.

Tip Tutors rarely use trick questions. If you think a question is a trick question, re-read and make sure that you thoroughly understand what you are reading before you answer.

Overcoming anxiety

Anxiety is a normal part of human life. A small amount can be a good thing because it improves alertness, readiness and concentration. However, a large amount of anxiety can have a negative effect, stopping us achieving our full potential.

If you feel that anxiousness may have a negative influence on your performance in tests and examinations, there are a number of ways to reduce the problem.

- **Build your personal confidence**. If you are struggling on your course and are becoming anxious about tests, you need to build your personal confidence. Speak to your tutor to obtain advice and guidance about how you can improve your study skills and academic performance. Once you begin to improve on your course, you will find that your anxiety about tests will be reduced.

- **Keep positive**. Think about how well you could do, rather than focus on how badly you might do (although you need to make sure that you don't place too much pressure on yourself to perform well). Don't think about bad test performances in the past and don't become distracted by the performance of friends and classmates.

- **Keep healthy in mind and body**. Try to keep relaxed through learning meditation techniques or learning to breathe slowly and deeply. Get plenty of sleep and exercise. Don't cram in too much revision. Eat a good breakfast before the test, and eat a healthy diet generally. Stress and anxiety can be made worse by lack of sleep, lack of exercise and poor diet (see Chapter 22).

- **Know what to expect**. If you know exactly what to expect from a test, you will be less anxious. Your tutor should provide more information and you may find it useful to speak to other students who have already taken this type of test. Try to visit the venue beforehand so that you are not met by any unpleasant surprises on the day of the test.

- **Arrive in good time**. Make sure that you know how long it takes to get to the venue and that you have checked how you will travel there. Rushing to a venue can increase anxiety levels considerably.

- **Don't panic**. When you take the test, try not to panic. Breathe slowly and deeply. Read each question carefully and fully. Try to concentrate on the questions and what you know, rather than your feelings of anxiety. Answer a question that you find easier so that you can feel more confident and reduce anxiety.

Summary

Students are required to take tests so that they can demonstrate their knowledge and understanding of their course as it progresses. Some tests are assessed, whereas others are informal, ungraded tests. Some tutors will schedule tests into the timetable and help you to prepare and plan for them, whereas others may spring a test on you, at any time during the course. Good preparation, organization, planning and constant revision will help you to succeed in your tests.

Some tutors use oral tests to test the knowledge and communication skills of their students. Other tutors ask their students to make oral presentations, which can be assessed or non-assessed. Information on how to make a successful presentation is provided in the following chapter.

21 Improving your presentation skills

Most students will have to make some kind of presentation during their studies. For university undergraduates and postgraduates this could be presenting a seminar or a conference paper, whereas for other students it may involve an individual or group presentation to other students on the course.

When making a presentation, good preparation and practice are essential. You also need to think about visual aids, your presentation style and controlling your nerves. These issues are discussed in this chapter. If you have to make a presentation as part of an oral test, more information is provided in Chapter 20.

Exercise

When you attend seminars, take note of how they are presented as this will help you to understand how to present your own seminar. Questions to ask include the following.

How does the presenter speak?

What does their body language say?

Do they vary their pitch and tone?

What hand and facial gestures do they use?

How do they present their information?

Is the information easy to understand or muddled and confused?

Do they hold your attention? If not, why not?

What visual aids do they use? Are they effective?

Is there anything you think the presenter could do better?

Presenting a seminar

The secret to presenting a good seminar is preparation. This will help you to control your nerves and you will feel more relaxed and confident. Also, if you know your subject well and show an interest, you will come across as professional and knowledgeable. Fellow students will be keen to listen to what you have to say and will be willing to participate in the discussion.

Preparing for your seminar

Through undertaking the above exercise you will begin to get a clearer idea of what works well and what you should avoid. You can then go on to prepare your own seminar. The following points will help in this preparation.

- Begin your preparation at least two weeks before the date of your seminar. This will give you a chance to read around the subject and follow up any issues that need clarification.

- Think about the type of handouts that you need to produce. For example, you might wish to give participants a copy of your seminar paper. This outlines all your ideas and arguments on the topic in a structured way, similar to an essay.

Some tutors will require you to produce a seminar paper that you must hand in as part of your assessed work.

▪ Tackle your seminar paper as you would a written assignment:

- identify key areas;

- begin reading;

- take notes;

- develop arguments;

- write a draft;

- rewrite;

- return to the reading if necessary;

- edit and proofread.

▪ Gather together your visual aids, or prepare your presentation using presentation software (see page 209). Produce a list of questions that you can ask to stimulate discussion once you have presented your seminar.

▪ Practise your talk. Time yourself to check that it lasts for the right amount of time.

Running your seminar

Before the seminar takes place make sure that you have with you all your handouts, visual aids, presentation software/ equipment and anything else you may require. Turn up early so that you can rearrange furniture, if required, and set up and test your equipment.

During the seminar speak clearly and confidently, slowing your speech and lowering your voice tone very slightly. This will help you to control any voice wobbles caused by nervousness.

Tip When you present a seminar you should not read straight from your paper as this is an ineffective method of presentation that can be boring for other members of the seminar group. Instead, you need to produce visual aids and/or a presentation that will help you to speak around the topic.

Presenting at a conference

Some postgraduate and undergraduate students may have to present a paper at a conference. Although this can seem daunting, with careful preparation and practice it can be a fulfilling and exciting experience.

Making a submission

For most conferences you will need to submit an abstract, a title, or a whole conference paper for acceptance. When doing this, find out exactly what is required. Make sure that you meet the brief and that your topic is relevant to the conference. Stick to all word limits provided by the conference organizer and ensure that your abstract/title/paper is submitted by the stated deadline.

If your submission is accepted, you should be sent more information about the style and structure of the conference. This should include information about the length and type of presentation. For example, some conferences will divide delegates into smaller groups and pair up presenters, perhaps for a one-hour time slot. Others might require presenters to speak to the whole conference, perhaps in a twenty-minute slot. If this information is not provided, contact the conference organizer.

Preparing your paper

When preparing your paper, try not to say too much. Most people have a fairly short attention span so you need to get across your most important and interesting points, without rambling. Keep your ideas focused and avoid too much jargon. All papers should include an introduction, middle and conclusion.

Tip Practise your paper in front of friends, in front of a mirror or tape yourself. Iron out any problems with your delivery and body language.

Presenting your paper

The following tips will help you to make your conference presentation.

- Try to view the room before you present your paper. You can check that all the required equipment and seating are available and it should help you to relax a little.

- If you have to use a microphone, make sure that it is properly adjusted to your height before you begin speaking.

- At most conferences it is perfectly acceptable to read out your paper, and this is useful if you are new to presentations of this type. However, try to make your reading interesting through tone variation. Use your voice for projection and inflection. Speak slowly and clearly.

- Make eye contact with members of the audience while you read (if it's a large audience, sweep your eyes across the room from time to time, to show that you are including everyone).

- Use visual aids (see below).

- Maintain a good posture, relax and breathe quietly and deeply. Have a glass of water with you.

- Don't worry about the size of the audience, and don't take things personally if only a few people turn up. This could be due to a variety of reasons, such as timing, simultaneous papers or your session being too early or too late in the day.

- Let your audience know whether you are happy to receive questions during, or after, your presentation. Answer all questions with courtesy and respect.

Using visual aids

Visual aids should be used in your presentation because they add interest and help to explain and illustrate the points that you are making. They also help to keep your audience's attention.

Today there are many types of visual aid that can be used by students who have to make presentations. These include pictures, photographs, slides, graphs, tables, props, flip charts, white/black boards, projectors and transparencies.

When using visual aids, you should take note of the following.

- Make sure that text is clear and large enough so that it can be read by all members of the audience. This is of particular importance if using OHP transparencies. Pay close attention to spelling, punctuation and grammar.

- If you are using photographs, pictures or slides, make sure that all images are clear enough to be seen by everybody. All sources must be fully acknowledged.

- If writing on a flip chart or board, stand to the side when writing and speaking, pay close attention to spelling and make sure that the board can be seen by all participants.

- Practise with all equipment prior to your presentation. Make sure that batteries/electric sockets are available and that your equipment is working. Have back-up visual aids available to cover unforeseen problems on the day.

'I won't use flip charts or black or white boards because my spelling is atrocious. I make sure I produce all visual aids beforehand so that I can check my spelling and won't show myself up during the presentation.'

Simon, freelance trainer

Using presentation software

Another option for your visual aids is presentation software. Contact your college/university IT services or speak to your tutor to find out what software is available for your use. Some colleges and universities will run training courses on how to use the software, and others have online tutorials available.

This software enables you to produce professional presentations, work together with others, organize and share your ideas, secure your work and measure the success of your presentation.

If you are interested in presentation software, you may find the following websites useful:

- SlideRocket (www.sliderocket.com);

- Prezi (http://prezi.com);

- Empressr (www.empressr.com);
- 280Slides (http://280slides.com);
- Vcasmo (http://vcasmo.com);
- PowerPoint (http://office.microsoft.com/powerpoint).

Tip If you are presenting at a conference, give your technology requirements to the conference organizer before the conference takes place. Check that these have been met when you arrive.

Producing handouts

Make sure that your audience is able to take away written information so that they can return to what you have said at a later date. Always include your name, contact e-mail address and the title of your paper on any handouts. If you are making a presentation to an outside organization, also include your college or university.

It is advisable to give your handouts to group/conference members at the end of your presentation. That way, people will not be distracted by reading your paper when you are talking. As with any written work, place close attention to structure, style, grammar, punctuation, spelling and presentation (see Chapters 4 and 5).

Overcoming nerves

Even the most experienced presenters get nervous when they make speeches. Often it is the extra amount of adrenalin produced that gets you through the presentation and makes it more interesting and animated.

The following points will help you to control your nerves when making a presentation.

- Talk about your concerns and worries with other students. Ask your tutor to discuss making presentations in class.

- Learn breathing techniques. When you breathe fully and deeply from your stomach you slow your breath automatically, which helps to control nerves and tension.

- Know your subject and practise your speech. It will help you to feel more confident.

- If possible, ask a friend to sit in your line of vision. They will be able to offer encouragement from the audience.

- Have water available during your presentation. This will help if your mouth dries or your throat begins to tickle.

- Slow down your speech and pitch your voice at a lower level. You are less likely to squeak or cough if you do this.

- Don't fear your audience as most, if not all, will be willing you to succeed.

'Even though I've been doing this for years I still get nervous at the start. So what I do is talk to people as soon as they arrive. It gets me used to the sound of my voice in that room. I also get people to introduce themselves when we first start, so that I'm not the only person speaking. It gives me chance to relax and gather my thoughts before I start my presentation.'

Simon, freelance trainer

Summary

As a student you may need to make a presentation on your course. This could include presenting a seminar or a conference paper, for example. Visual aids add interest to your presentation, and help to clarify the points that you are making. Handouts should be provided so that your audience can take away a record of what has been said.

Many people get nervous about making presentations. These nerves can be reduced through careful preparation and planning. You will also find that your nerves are reduced if you maintain health, learn to relax and cope with stress. These issues are discussed in the following chapter.

22 Increasing your chances of success

You will be able to increase your chances of success on your course if you take note of all the study skills information provided so far in this book. In addition to this, there is other action that you can take to improve your chances of success. This includes maintaining health, coping with stress, creating the right environment, setting goals, building motivation and recognizing the skills that you gain from your course. These issues are discussed in this chapter.

Maintaining health

Your health should be maintained at levels suitable to aid your studies. Poor health can affect your ability to complete coursework; for example, by preventing you from attending lectures and lowering your motivation to work independently. Everyday tasks become harder and more stressful and social relationships begin to suffer.

Taking action to improve health

The following tips will help you to improve your health and well-being.

- Maintaining a good diet is essential to your health and well-being.

- Cook your own meals (where possible), using fresh, healthy ingredients. Two good cookbooks for students are listed at the end of this chapter.
- Eat plenty of fresh fruit and vegetables and limit fat and salt in your cooking.
- If you are eating in catered halls or canteens, try to vary what you eat.
- Avoid junk food as it will be kinder on your pocket and on your health.
- Always eat breakfast and don't skip other meals.

■ Get plenty of sleep.
- Avoid stimulants such as alcohol, coffee and nicotine before you go to bed.
- Limit the number of late nights.
- Go to bed and get up at similar times during the working week. Your body will become used to the routine and you will find it easier to fall asleep at night and get up in the morning.

■ Get plenty of exercise as it is good for your health and will help you to sleep.
- Join a sports club.
- Take advantage of free facilities at your college/ university.
- Walk where possible.

■ Avoid marathon study sessions.
- Take plenty of breaks and move your limbs frequently.
- Don't work when you should be sleeping.

'Joining the netball team was great. I met new friends, got loads of exercise and went out every Wednesday night for a few drinks with the rest of the team and with the men from the rugby team.'

Paula, Southampton

Coping with stress

Stress is defined as a physical, mental or emotional factor that causes bodily or mental tension. Some of the symptoms of the condition are listed in Table 5. However, these symptoms can be due to other medical conditions so, if you are concerned about any problems, you should consult your doctor.

Table 5. Symptoms of stress.

Physical	Psychological	Behavioural
Skin rashes	Mood swings	Over and under eating
Lump in the throat	Worrying unreasonably	Working extra and long hours
Tickling cough	Excessive concern about physical health	Unreasonable complaining
Pain or tightness in chest	Constant withdrawal	Accident proneness
Palpitations	Tiredness	Poor work, cheating and evasion
Frequent indigestion	Lack of concentration	Increased dependency on drugs
Stomach pains or diarrhoea	Increased anxiety	Careless driving
Muscle tension, neck, shoulder or back pain	Increased irritability	Change in sleep patterns
Persistent headaches	Excessive daydreaming	Increased absenteeism
Double vision or difficulty focusing eyes	Inability to feel sympathy for others	Delayed recovery from accidents and illnesses

Reducing stress levels

If you are suffering from stress the following tips may help you to cope.

- Talk about your problems and anxieties with family, friends and/or tutors.

- Be selective in your tasks and drop everything that is not essential.

- Work out why you are tense and worried. Alter the situation that is causing the trouble.

- Think through stressful events before they happen. Be well prepared.

- Recognize that you don't have to be a perfectionist all the time.

- Don't criticize yourself, or others, too much.

- Avoid competition and try to cultivate co-operation instead. Gaining support from other students will help with your studies and your personal life. Don't fret about getting lower marks than someone else on your course.

- Escape from your worries for a while and take a break if possible. Use vacations wisely and relax. Don't spend the whole holiday fretting over work.

- Allocate yourself recreation time and make sure that you use it.

- Overcome anger and frustration with physical activity.

Tip Yoga and meditation are excellent ways to reduce stress. Courses can be run by colleges, universities, adult education centres, local community centres or freelance trainers.

Seeking help

There are a number of people employed in colleges and universities to help students who are suffering from stress (and other conditions).

- **Welfare services**. Many college and university students' unions run an advice and welfare service for their members. As a student you can register to become a member of the students' union and use their free welfare service.

- **Counselling services**. Many universities employ their own student counsellor, and if they don't, the welfare services will be able to put you in touch with an outside counsellor. University counselling services are free to students.

- **Medical facilities**. Most universities and some larger colleges have their own medical centre on campus. Appointments with doctors and nurses can be arranged on campus and an emergency number is provided for evenings and weekends.

- **Religious services**. Many universities and colleges have their own chaplain and religious advisers, representing a variety of faiths. Some will hold full-time appointments within the student community whereas others are part-time and hold congregations elsewhere.

Tip Campus doctors and counsellors are trained to deal with the types of health problems faced by students. If you are ever in any doubt about any condition you are experiencing, always seek professional advice.

Creating a working environment

You will increase your chances of success if you are able to find or create a good working environment. When doing so, consider the following.

▪ Ensure that your working space is free from distractions. Set ground rules from the start and make sure that parents, partners, siblings and friends know that you need quiet study time and should not be disturbed.

▪ Keep your personal working space neat, well organized and well stocked (see page 220), so that you have everything to hand and can find items quickly.

▪ All important work will need to be left alone or tidied away where it cannot be disturbed by others. This is of particular importance if other people are to use your working space or PC/laptop.

▪ Try to meet the health and safety guidelines listed opposite.

Gathering resources

You will find it easier to get down to your studies, and remain motivated, if you have all the necessary resources close to hand. What you will need depends on the type, subject and level of your course, and the amount of equipment and books provided by your college or university.

All students will need to obtain some or all of the following.

▪ Key textbooks. Speak to your tutor to find out which are key texts. Find out how many of these are available in your college or university library. Work out whether it would be beneficial to buy your own copy, and if you are on a low budget, think about buying a second-hand copy.

Health and safety guidelines

There must be plenty of light. Natural daylight is best, but if you intend to work during the evenings ensure that you have good lighting that does not produce glare or shadows on your books, paper or screen.

The room should have good, natural ventilation.

Your desk needs to be big enough to allow for all your computing equipment and provide space for your paperwork.

The top of your computer screen should be at eye level or slightly lower.

The viewing distance of your screen should be 45–60 centimetres.

Your screen should be free of glare, shadows and reflections.

Your mouse should be placed level with your keyboard and near enough so that you don't have to stretch.

You should keep frequently used items within easy reach.

Your chair should be at a height that allows a 90° angle at your elbows for typing.

You should be able to sit with your thighs horizontal, your lower legs vertical and your feet flat on the floor or on a footrest.

The seat should swivel and have a padded, curved seat.

The back of the chair should offer firm support and you should be able to sit upright with your back on the lumbar support without the seat cutting into the back of your knees.

There should be plenty of leg room.

Take frequent breaks and move your limbs on a regular basis.

- Stationery. This includes paper, pens, pencils, notepads, ring binders, hole punch, document pouches, file dividers, staples and refills. These can be bought cheaply from your students' union shop once you arrive at college/university, or from office supply stores or online. Buying in bulk can work out cheaper, so buy with friends once at college to cut costs.

- IT equipment. Most of your IT needs can be met by your college/university. However, if you prefer to buy your own equipment think about what you need. Choose hardware and software that are required for your course; this will help with your coursework and study skills, and it will save you time, money and brainwork.

Tip Remember to obtain insurance for any expensive IT equipment that you take to college/university.

Setting goals

In relation to your course a goal is a clear statement that describes what you will be able to do at the end of your studies. This will include specific behaviour and a clear outcome. If you set clear goals at the beginning of your course you will find it easier to remain motivated (see below) and will feel more in control of your studies.

When setting goals keep them simple, set clear deadlines and write them down, keeping a list that you can refer to when required. Understand what action you need to take to meet your goals and try not to become too distracted. Celebrate when you achieve your goals.

'I help students to set goals at the beginning of the course. We refer to the course literature, the learner outcomes, and I get students to

*think about their own goals in relation to these. Students soon under-
stand what they are trying to achieve and are very happy when they
achieve it.'*

Anne, Bournemouth University

Building motivation

You will find it easier to build motivation if you enjoy your subject and are interested in what you are learning. Therefore,
you should make careful choices about which modules to
study. Don't choose modules purely because you think they
will be good for a job, or because your parents will approve,
for example.

It is also important to enjoy the way that your course is taught.
Try to choose modules that enable you to learn in a way that
suits your learning style (see Chapter 1) although this may not
always be possible. Set goals (see previous page) and make
challenges for yourself. Read around subjects and study
independently (see Chapter 9). Become active in the learning
process. Don't just accept information passively from your
tutor.

Gaining transferable skills

It is easier to remain motivated and achieve success if you are
able to see the personal benefits that you are gaining from
your course. You can do this by recognizing the development
of your transferable skills. These are skills that you develop
while you are away at college or university (and during life in
general) that can be transferred easily to the world of work.

Employers are keen to see that you have developed, and are
aware of, such skills. They are not interested solely in
the knowledge that you have gained from your course, but are

interested also in any skills and attributes that will help you to carry out your job effectively and make you a valuable member of the workforce.

Examples of skills that you could develop during your course include:

- organization skills;
- time-management;
- the ability to meet deadlines/set goals;
- the ability to work under pressure;
- crisis management;
- adaptability and flexibility;
- independent work/study skills;
- skills of reflection;
- problem-solving skills;
- skills of analysis, evaluation and synthesis;
- reviewing and critiquing skills;
- communication skills (verbal and written);
- editing/proofreading skills;
- IT skills;
- numerical skills;
- reading skills;
- research skills;
- presentation skills;
- teamworking skills;
- social skills;
- listening skills;
- the ability to empathize/support others.

Tip Keep a learning diary as this is the best way to recognize and record the skills that you are developing as your course progresses. It will be a useful source of information when you need to provide details of your skills on job application forms.

Summary

You can increase your chances of success on your course by making sure that you remain fit and healthy, control levels of stress and build motivation. To do this, choose courses and modules that are of personal interest and make sure that you set clear, achievable goals. You will further improve your chances of success by taking note of all the advice and guidance offered in this book.

The appendices offer some useful study skills tips, information about study skills support, listings of study skills software and websites, and conclude with further reading. I hope that you have enjoyed reading this book and that you find it useful on your course. I wish you every success with your studies.

Further reading

Crook, S., *The Survival Guide to Cooking in the Student Kitchen: And the house-sharing experience!* (Slough: Foulsham, 2008).

Humphries, C., *The New Students' Cook Book* (Slough: Foulsham, 2009).

Appendix 1
Study skills tips

The following list provides a quick reference to some of the most useful study skills tips for students.

- Understand how you learn. Take note of times when successful learning has taken place and when learning has not been successful. Be aware of factors that can distract you from learning (see Chapter 1).

- Learn how to manage your study time, plan your work, organize your studies and maximize productivity (see Chapter 2).

- Understand how to read effectively and know how and where to find good, reliable sources of information. Don't believe everything you read, but learn how to analyse and critique information that you find (see Chapters 3, 8 and 9).

- Find out how to structure assignments and make sure that written work is presented well, free from mistakes and pitched at the correct level. All work should be well referenced. Understand what is meant by plagiarism and copyright, and make sure that you don't breach the rules (see Chapters 4, 5 and 6).

- Listen to tutor feedback. Learn from their comments (see Chapter 7).

- Learn how to study independently. Keep your motivation levels high by setting and meeting goals and choosing modules that interest you (see Chapters 9 and 22).

- Learn to work with others. Try to co-operate rather than compete. Learn how to listen to others and know how to communicate well in groups (see Chapters 7 and 15).

- Organize, review and revise your work as your course progresses. Take time after each class/lecture to think about the topics that have been raised. Read around subjects and discuss topics with fellow students. If you are unsure of anything, ask your tutor for clarification (see Chapter 14).

- Become familiar with the latest IT equipment and information that is available to enhance your studies. This includes college/university hardware, software, online tools, podcasts, intranets, virtual learning environments and college/university websites (see Chapters 12 and 13).

- Don't panic about tests and examinations. Learn how to revise and prepare effectively. Make sure that you have all the required resources to hand and that you know what to expect (see Chapters 19 and 20).

- Seek help when required. Read this book, speak to your tutor, visit your college/university study support unit or enrol on additional training courses (see Appendix 2).

Appendix 2
Study skills support

Members of staff in universities and colleges understand that students need good academic support. As a consequence, there is a wide variety of learner support services available for students in colleges and universities. As a student you are entitled to use all of these services and most will be free of charge.

Services may include study support units, study support sessions, individual workshops, training courses and IT help and advice. Visit individual college/university websites, or consult the relevant prospectus, to find out what learner support facilities are available at your institution.

Using study support units

Many colleges and universities have a study support unit or a learner support unit that is available to help students with basic skills in reading, writing and numeracy. If you feel that you are struggling with any of these skills you can arrange to attend special sessions with a fully trained tutor.

These are held within the unit and will be arranged to suit your course timetable. In addition to these sessions, you can access learning resources and materials, computing facilities and other technological aids. Advice from supportive, trained staff is available when required. The aim of these units is to give you the skills and confidence to move on in your studies until you no longer need the support of the unit.

Most units will have 'drop-in' sessions during which you can seek general or specialist advice. This can be useful when you need help with something that may be short-term and quite specific. Consult college/university websites or contact the unit direct for information about opening times and drop-in sessions.

Developing your individual learning plan

At some study support units you will have a confidential interview with a learning support tutor. This could include a discussion covering:

- the problems you are facing on your course;
- your strengths and weaknesses;
- your hopes and fears;
- your educational experiences in the past and how these might relate to the problems you are facing.

Together you will develop an individual learning plan that will lay out your aims and objectives, so that you can set realistic goals for the short and long term.

The learner support tutor will focus on information relevant to your course, which makes the help you receive more interesting, relevant and useful. Some tutors will liaise with your course tutor to ensure that they give you the best possible help. The learner support tutor will work with you until you no longer require his or her help.

Enrolling on study support sessions

Many colleges and universities offer study support sessions for students who would like extra help with study skills such as essay writing, note-taking, presentation skills and revision techniques. A timetable of sessions is drawn up each semester/term.

The sessions are free to students and you can choose which sessions to attend. They are led by an experienced tutor and time may be set aside at the end for individual students to raise questions. Consult your college/university intranet/VLE or speak to your tutor to find out what sessions are available and to book a place.

Sheffield Hallam University has around 4,500 students who study part time. Many of these students study during the evenings because they are in full-time employment. This means that they are unable to access study skills support that is offered during the working week. Therefore, the university has set up extra weekend sessions that allow students to drop in for help with their academic work and study skills. Tutors are also more flexible when it comes to assignment deadlines for students who have employment or family commitments.

Enrolling on training courses

Some colleges and universities run extra training and workshops in subjects that may not have direct relevance to your course, but which may be of personal interest to you or useful for future careers. This may include sessions in counselling skills, interview techniques, compiling CVs and assertiveness, for example.

Many of these sessions will be free for students, although places are often limited so you need to book early. Contact the student and staff development team, human resource department or student enterprise centre at your college or university for more information.

Newport Business School, part of the University of Wales, Newport, offers twelve study skills modules to new students. They are focused on introductory issues, such as how to write essays. Students are able to work through the modules before they start the formal part of the course. The modules were introduced because many students were arriving at the university without the ability to study at the deeper knowledge level required for undergraduate work, even though they had received the required grades.

Obtaining IT support

All colleges and universities will offer IT help and support to their students. Some have set up an IT support centre or a learner support centre to offer advice specifically on IT use. Others have a computing department or IT helpdesk that will offer information, advice and guidance to students. Contact details and opening hours will be available on your college/ university website or intranet.

Obtaining disability support

Some of the bigger colleges and universities have a special office or department that deals with disability issues. Details of these offices can be obtained from university websites or prospectuses.

Most institutions employ disability officers or advisers who ensure that students with disabilities receive all the help and support they need. Support and facilities vary, but institutions should have accessible rooms, specialist equipment, note-takers, advisers and support workers. They should also be able to provide living accommodation that meets your needs.

Examination arrangements

Your disability adviser will be able to help you with any alternative examination arrangements that you may require. These depend on your individual needs and may include:

- additional time and extra reading time;
- rest breaks;
- flexible starting time;
- personal assistance, such as a scribe, reader or interpreter;
- specialist equipment, such as computers, dictionaries and furniture;
- large print, Braille or audio-tape exam papers;
- a separate venue.

Applying for disability funding

Another role of the disability adviser is to help you with your application for Disabled Students' Allowances (DSA). These are funds set up by the government to help with extra costs you may have to pay as a result of your disability if you want to study at higher education level. They are not available for study at further education level.

Appendix 3
Study skills software

There is a wide variety of software available to help support students with their study skills. Some examples are provided below. However, it is not possible to provide a list of all the software that is available. Therefore, contact your college/university IT services or study support unit to find out what is available for your use, or visit the websites listed below for more information and to download free applications.

Free open-source software packages

Visit Wikipedia (http://en.wikipedia.org) and enter 'list of free and open source software packages' into the search box. This page provides you with a comprehensive list of all the software and online tools that are freely available, including science, mathematics, computing and learning support software. Descriptions of each entry are provided, along with links to relevant websites.

www.openoffice.org

Open Office is an open-source office software suite for word processing, spreadsheets, presentations, graphics, databases, etc. It works on all common computers and can be downloaded and used free of charge for any purpose.

Free online note-taking applications

- Evernote (www.evernote.com) enables you to store notes, web pages, links, photos, etc. Everything you capture is processed, indexed and made searchable automatically.

- 3banana Notes (https://snaptic.com) is available for Android, iPhone, and the web and enables you to capture and share your thoughts, ideas, notes and photos.

Reading and writing support

Texthelp Systems Ltd (www.texthelp.com) provides software to support students with their reading, writing and research skills at school, college, university and home. It is aimed at students who struggle with their reading and writing, such as those with literacy difficulties, dyslexia and where English is a second language.

- Read&Write GOLD is designed to assist students and individuals of all ages who require extra assistance when reading or composing text.

- Fluency Tutor is an online solution to help build and measure oral reading fluency.

- Lexiflow is a secure solution for creating accessible Adobe Flash talking eBooks and assessments for students who require read aloud support.

- Browsealoud is designed to improve website accessibility for those who struggle to read content online.

Bibliographic software

The packages listed below enable you to create, store, search and update your personal library of references. The software is also useful for helping you to summarize references (your summary is searchable so that you can find useful articles, even if you cannot remember the author or title). You can save PDFs of useful articles and link to relevant websites.

- Scholar's Aid (www.scholarsaid.com)
- RefWorks (www.refworks.com)
- EndNote (www.endnote.com)
- Reference Manager (www.refman.com)
- ProCite (www.procite.com)

Revision tools

More information about online revision tools can be obtained from the following websites.

- www.revisionworld.co.uk (for GCSE and A Level students)
- http://getrevising.co.uk (all levels and qualifications)
- www.bbc.co.uk/schools/bitesize (for GCSE and A Level students)

In addition to these online learning tools there is a useful free revision and examination unit provided by the Open University ('Revision and examinations'). Visit http://openlearn.open.ac.uk for more information and to access this course.

Online presentation tools and software

Online presentation tools and software enable you to produce professional presentations, work together with others, organize and share your presentations, secure your work and measure the success of your presentation. Visit the following websites for more information about these tools.

- SlideRocket (www.sliderocket.com);
- Prezi (http://prezi.com);
- Empressr (www.empressr.com);
- 280Slides (http://280slides.com);
- Vcasmo (http://vcasmo.com);
- PowerPoint (http://office.microsoft.com/powerpoint).

Appendix 4
Study skills websites

www.open.ac.uk/skillsforstudy

This section of the Open University website provides useful study skills information, covering topics such as assignments, revision, examinations, maths and statistics. Information is aimed at university students.

www.bbc.co.uk/skillswise

Visit this BBC website for information, advice, tips and exercises that will help you to improve your grammar, spelling, reading, listening, writing and vocabulary skills. This website provides useful information for school pupils and college students.

www.bbc.co.uk/schools

This BBC website provides information for school pupils, including revision and exam skills. It also includes important information on stress and health.

www.bbc.co.uk/raw

This BBC site provides practical help and advice for everyday life skills, such as using computers, managing your money or writing a CV.

www.videojug.com

Visit the 'family and education' section of this site for videos from lecturers and tutors about attending lectures, seminars and tutorials. There are also videos on taking exams, writing essays and improving concentration. Information is available for school, college and university students.

www.ltscotland.org.uk

Learning and Teaching Scotland is funded by the Scottish government. This site provides study skills information for school pupils aged 5–18. It includes information about essay writing, learning styles, memory skills, note-taking and reading.

www.move-on.org.uk

If you have problems with your basic English and maths skills, you can visit this website to try a numeracy and literacy test, and to find out more about what help is available locally.

Appendix 5
Study skills books

Cottrell, S., *The Study Skills Handbook* (3rd edition, Basingstoke: Palgrave Macmillan, 2008).

Dawson, C., *Introduction to Research Methods* (4th edition, Oxford: How To Books, 2009).

Elliot, J. and Marsh, C., *Exploring Data: An introduction to data analysis for social scientists* (2nd edition, Cambridge: Polity Press, 2008).

Hennessy, B. *Writing an Essay: Simple techniques to transform your coursework and examinations* (5th edition, Oxford: How To Books 2007).

Holtorn, E., *Study Skills* (Tenterden: Galore Park Publishing Ltd, 2007).

Leech, G. et al., *An A-Z of English Grammar and Usage* (Harlow: Pearson Education Ltd, 2009).

Levin, P., *Successful Teamwork! For undergraduates and taught postgraduates working on group projects* (Maidenhead: Open University Press, 2004).

Swetnam, D., *Writing Your Dissertation: The bestselling guide to planning, preparing and presenting first-class work* (3rd edition, revised and updated, Oxford: How To Books Ltd, 2004).

Weyers, J. and McMillan, K., *How to Write Essays and Assignments* (Harlow: Pearson Education, 2007).

Index